DOCUMENTATION STANDARDS AND PROCEDURES FOR ONLINE SYSTEMS

DOCUMENTATION STANDARDS AND PROCEDURES FOR ONLINE SYSTEMS

EDITED BY

MARTIN L. RUBIN

 VAN NOSTRAND REINHOLD COMPANY

NEW YORK   CINCINNATI   ATLANTA   DALLAS   SAN FRANCISCO
LONDON   TORONTO   MELBOURNE

Van Nostrand Reinhold Company Regional Offices:
New York Cincinnati Atlanta Dallas San Francisco

Van Nostrand Reinhold Company International Offices:
London Toronto Melbourne

Library of Congress Catalog Card Number: 78-14038
ISBN : 0-442-80042-8

Manufactured in the United States of America

Published by Van Nostrand Reinhold Company
135 West 50th Street, New York, NY 10020

Published simultaneously in Canada by Van Nostrand Reinhold Ltd.

15 14 13 12 11 10 9 8 7 6 5 4 3 2

Library of Congress Cataloging in Publication Data

Main entry under title:

Documentation standards and procedures for online systems.

    Includes index.
    1. On-line data processing—Standards.
I. Rubin, Martin L. II. Knetsch, Marilyn.
QA76.55.S7   001.6'4404   78-14038
ISNB 0-442-80042-8

Contributors:
Jerome Gitomer
Ellis R. Cash
Charles Lamb
Beverly Hunter

Technical Editor:
Marilyn Knetsch

Assistant Editors:
Leila Spevak
Ida Pearson

In memory of

MARILYN B. KNETSCH

Her life was one of dedication, love, and inspiration. She always strove for perfection in everything she did. This marked her efforts as technical editor of this and previous works. She was a ceaseless worker and dedicated to all who knew her.

PREFACE

This book is the culmination of many years' work in the conceptualization and development of standards and procedures for modern online systems. It represents the combined thinking and work of a number of individuals, companies, and organizations, all of whom contributed to the work. It is a first step in the development of a comprehensive set of procedures for online system development and operation. However, it is a significant leap forward from current standards and procedures which are based on a batch orientation. We anticipate that you and your organization will make many modifications to these procedures as you adapt them to your unique environment and organization.

We solicit and encourage the readers of this book to submit to the editor, Martin L. Rubin, extensions and modifications of these procedures, for use in an update scheduled for Spring, 1982. Acknowledgment will be made of the author of any materials published, with sub-royalties possible. Please mail the original of such materials to Martin L. Rubin, 121 Bay Colony Drive, Virginia Beach. Va. 23451.

The editor of this book would like to especially acknowledge the contribution of Synoptic Systems Corporation, Falls Church, Va.[*] This corporation developed for the Federal Trade Commission a number of ideas in the areas of structured design and documentation, as well as simplification of computer operations and procedures, which have been incorporated into this book. Dick Thomas, Vice President of Synoptic Systems Corporation, offered support, guidance, and directions in the formulation of standards for use by the Federal Trade Commission, which was instrumental in developing these standards.

The work of Jerome Gitomer, who was one of the initial participants in the conceptualization of this work, is gratefully acknowledged.

The participation of Beverly Hunter, who contributed to the development of standards for man-machine dialogues, is gratefully acknowledged.

Leila Spevak and Ida Pearson, Assistant Technical Editors, were superb in their response to the call of editing the final manuscript in a short time frame to meet publisher deadlines.

MARTIN L. RUBIN

[*]We would also like to acknowledge the contribution of American Management Systems, Inc. for their ideas on standards planning guidelines in hardware resource estimation and cost-benefit analysis.

INTRODUCTION

The standards and procedures contained in this work are organized in a manner that facilitates their use. We have found through research that standards which are in one inseparable document are difficult to use by the standards' holder. These standards are designed so that the user may refer to the particular subject which he will reference on that day; e.g., documentation guideline or job control procedures.

The standards are organized as follows: There are major standards groupings and individual stand-alone standards within each grouping. Each practice has a complete title and identification.

Nearly every organization that uses this book will have some standards in one form or another. Therefore, a choice will have to be made as to whether to convert existing standards into the organizational format of this work, or to select individual groupings and standards within this work, for adaptation to the format of existing standards. We recommend the former approach since it will force the organization to review all existing standards as they are converted into the new organization.

The single major word of caution is the problem of whether the standards will be enforced and used by the data processing organization personnel. We have found that many organizations pay lip service to standards and procedures and the manual gathers dust on people's desks.

In the development of this work, a special effort was made to pay attention to the practicality of the standards contained herein:

- Are they workable?
- Will the staff be willing to use them?
- What will it cost in staff time to adhere to these standards?

The best approach is to solicit the opinion of key personnel about the proposed standards. Then, in the final analysis, management must decide the importance of enforcing particular procedures.

In developing these standards, one of our major difficulties was the problem of whether we could provide specific procedures or general guidelines for conducting work activities. In our earliest attempt, our approach was to be as detailed as possible in all areas. This was found to be not feasible since the specific hardware and software environment and staff organization will determine the exact nature of the standards and procedures that are required.

After decisions have been made regarding the format to be used, a review must be made of each set of practices contained in this work for possible adoption in the company procedures. Secondly, a review should be made of changes in individual standards that will make them suitable for your organization's use. This review may include the decision to adopt only the concepts of the standard or a portion of the content, or to expand the current content with specific detail.

We consider this book a starting point in the development of standards which are tailored to online systems. We hope that it will inspire organizations to review their existing standards and procedures, and initiate major revisions. We hope that this process of change will be shared with future readers in the update of this work, as we have noted in the Preface.

The standards contained in this book assume an IBM 360/370 hardware and software environment. We realize that many readers will have a variety of new generation hardware and software produced by many different vendors. We would greatly appreciate receiving, and will be pleased to consider for publication, any procedures developed by readers for other hardware/ software environments.

COMPARING BATCH AND ONLINE SYSTEM STANDARDS

Standards written for batch systems are inappropriate for online applications. From a systems viewpoint there is a fundamental differnece between the online real time system and the conventional batch system. The online system's operator interacts with the computer as events take place, while the batch system reports on events that have already transpired. Thus, the standards for each system must be completely different.

Major conceptual differences between the two types of systems are:

CHARACTERISTIC	ONLINE	BATCH
Basic processing unit	Transaction	Group of related transactions
Availability	Continuous	Scheduled time only
Input source stream	Unrelated types	Related groups only
Input controller	User	Computer program control
Input data rate	Unpredictable	Constant
Input presentation	Parallel	Serial
Response time	Seconds	Hours
Basic process objective	Complete transaction	Process group
Optimized for	User	Central processor
Environment	Dynamic	Static
System control	Multi-level	Single level
Input sources	Many	Few
Reliability	Critical	Less critical

The basic processing unit of the online system is the transaction, often called the message. The online system processes one transaction at a time through a series of functions required to complete it. In contrast, the batch system processes an entire set of transactions, one function at a time.

An online system must be readily available to users at any time of day or night. A batch system output is available to the users on a scheduled basis. The output for the online system is controlled by the user and is presented to the system by the user, who is not under the control of the data processing department. By contrast, the input to the batch system is controlled by the computer operator, who can present it to the system at the time which best suits the convenience of the data processing operations staff.

The online system must be designed so that the processing required for any given transaction cannot be determined until after it has been submitted by the user, and examined by the system. In the batch system, the operator accumulates groups, or batches, of related transactions and presents them to the system. The online system must therefore have a control structure for calling in appropriate modules, while the batch system need only have the logic necessary to recognize that the transactions are in the correct format for acceptance by a program.

The user controls the input. Nothing happens until he submits a transaction for processing. It is not possible to predict when, what, or where the user will submit input to the system. In the batch system, the operating system scheduler controls when the data will be processed and from which device.

Online systems must be able to handle more than one transaction at a time because there would be an unreasonable delay if transactions were processed serially. This requires that the system have a priority interrupt capability and queues to hold in-process transactions. The batch system (because the program controls the reading of data) handles one transaction at a time.

The response time of the online system is measured in seconds, or fractions of a second, because it interacts with a human operator who functions in real time. It accepts a message, places it in an input queue, retrieves it from the queue, determines its type, edits it, and responds to the user with another question, a format, error message, etc. When dealing with human operators, the response time must be compatible with their processing speed and reaction time.

The environment of the online system is a dynamic one: users request services and are constantly competing for the communications facilities. Therefore the workload cannot be fully predicted in advance, and the system must provide satisfactory response times during peak periods.

In additon to the more demanding nature of the online system, more hardware is required to support it: remote terminals, a communications network, controllers, modems, fast direct access storage, etc.

Online systems have a lower tolerance for failure than do batch systems. When a batch system fails, the schedule is disrupted and some deadlines are missed, but when an online system fails, the organization cannot process the incoming data, and many of the operating functions of the business are affected. Restart and recovery procedures therefore must allow users to pick up where they left off before the system crash. In some cases it is necessary to continue processing even with component failures.

The problem is to recognize the fundamental differences between batch and online processing, and then to determine their impact on the organization's procedures, documentation requirements, etc.

The standards in this book have been especially devised to reflect the various aspects of an online system. A comparison of the elements of a batch, versus online standard manual, is shown below:

BATCH	ONLINE
Pre-processing	Transaction logic
Keypunch instructions	Man-machine dialogue
Program flowcharts	Screen formats
File definitions	Input codes
Record layouts	Command syntax
Program documentation	Module documentation
Console operator documentation (run book)	Data base organization
Input forms	Data base access method
Output forms	Communications queues
Report distribution lists	Security tables
	Communications line control
	File directories
	Communication network layouts
	Terminal specification
	Terminal operator instructions
	Transaction logs
	Linkage records

CONTENTS

PREFACE   v
INTRODUCTION   vii

Series   Practice

0100   PROJECT PLANNING AND REVIEW   1
    0110   User Request   3
    0120   Cost Estimate Request   7
    0130   Feasibility Study   11
    0140   Identification Standards   16
    0150   Cost-Benefit Analysis Guideline   20
    0160   Hardware Resource Requirement Estimate   34

0200   SYSTEM DEVELOPMENT   43
    0210   Structured Development Methodology Guideline   45
    0220   System Development Cycle Documentation Guideline   52
    0230   Structured COBOL Guideline   64
    0240   Edit and Validation Specification   74
    0250   Current System Summary   83
    0260   System Test Plan   98

0300   DOCUMENTATION AIDS   101
    0310   Short HIPO Documentation Guideline   103
    0320   Data Correlation and Documentation System   119

0400   OPERATIONS   131
    0410   Job Control Language Standards   133
    0420   Production Control Run Book   145
    0430   Terminal Operator's Manual   150

0500   DATA BASE   159
    0510   Data Base Administrator   161
    0520   Data Base Requirements Document   170
    0530   Data Dictionary   182
    0540   Data Base Organization   186

0600   MAN MACHINE DIALOGUE   201
    0610   Dialogue Specifications   203

0700   DATA COMMUNICATIONS   213
    0710   Communications Requirements Document   215
    0720   Communications Specifications   225
    0730   Terminal Requirements Document   242

            INDEX   249

DOCUMENTATION STANDARDS AND PROCEDURES FOR ONLINE SYSTEMS

project planning and review

PRACTICE 0100
USER REQUEST

CONTENTS

I. INTRODUCTION

    A. GENERAL
    B. PURPOSE

II. USER REQUEST FORM

    A. DATE SUBMITTED
    B. DATE REQUIRED
    C. MANHOURS AUTHORIZED:
       MACHINE HOURS AUTHORIZED
    D. DO NOT FILL IN
    E. INFORMATION AVAILABLE
    F. SPECIAL CONSIDERATIONS

FIGURE 1: USER REQUEST

I. INTRODUCTION

A. GENERAL

This practice describes a form that is to be utilized in all service requests to the ADP organization.

B. PURPOSE

The service request form is a formal procedure for requesting ADP service, which briefly summarizes the work to be performed and information about that work.

II. USER REQUEST FORM

A user request for service is shown in Figure 1. On this form, the user briefly describes the computer application or other service desired.

Job No.	USER REQUEST	Do Not Fill In

Job No. _____

USER REQUEST

Work Req. No.: ___ —
main   sub

Problem Title: _____

Rec'd. by:

Originator: _____

Dept./Sec.: _____ Ext.: _____

Person Assigned:

Date Submitted: ___/___/___ Date Required: ___/___/___

Dept./Sec. Assigned:

Manhours   Machine Hrs.
Authorized: _____ Authorized: _____

Date Rec'd.:   /   /

Authorized Signature: _____

Date Closed: /   /

NATURE OF WORK (check one):

☐ Feasibility Study

☐ Emergency Program Maintenance

☐ New System Development

☐ Special Study

☐ New System Automation

☐ Other: _____

☐ Complex System Modification

_____

☐ Simple System Modification

_____

WORK DESCRIPTION (Problem area, application, requirements, etc.):

INFORMATION AVAILABLE (List documents attached or available):

SPECIAL CONSIDERATIONS (Such as, new equipment, monetary limitations, priority needs, other comments):

Figure 1. User request.

Selected entries on the form are discussed below:

A. DATE SUBMITTED

Submit the User Request as far in advance as possible. The Automatic Data Processing (ADP) staff workload is highly variable and backlogs occur frequently—advance scheduling of new work is a must.

B.   DATE REQUIRED

Insert a realistic date. For example, a request for a complex new program, submitted on the 15th of the month for delivery on the 30th, is not realistic.

The DP supervisor is obligated to inform the user if he thinks the date required cannot be met.

If repetitive services are required, write "Open" in the *Date Required* position.

C.   MANHOURS AUTHORIZED: MACHINE HOURS AUTHORIZED

Either or both of these authorizations will establish the limit(s) to the time granted to do the work. If the supervisor judges the time limit(s) inadequate, he will inform the user before beginning the work.

Unless the time required for the job can be estimated with some assurance, the ADP department should be consulted as to whether a Request for Cost Estimate (see Practice 0120) is appropriate.

D.   DO NOT FILL IN

The ADP department personnel receiving the User Request shall fill in the areas under this heading, *except:*

Where the first User Request in a series has been designated "Open" as to Date Required and has had a User Request Number assigned, then the Originator fills in the User Request Number using the "main" number previously assigned, and inserting as the "sub" portion of it that number of the series of the repetitive work. Thus, if this is the seventh in a series of user requests of an open series under the main User Request No. 1518, the Originator inserts "1518" as the main number and "007" as the subnumber.

Beginning with the second user request in an open series, a Date Required, commensurate with the processing time taken on the first user request, is filled in.

The Authorized Signature is required only on the first user request of an open series. A typical example of the use of an open series of user requests would be in the case of repetitive production runs.

E.   INFORMATION AVAILABLE

The user should give his attention here to informing the analyst of pertinent manuals, write-ups, exhibits, etc., which are known to the user but may not be known to the analyst; e.g., bank teller manual, teller; repairman's self-instruction manual.

F. SPECIAL CONSIDERATIONS

Cite other pertinent information as the form indicates, such as "A principal criterion for selecting a winning proposal will be cutting the price and delivery date;" or "The time from entry of request to receipt of reply must be less than three seconds."

PRACTICE 0120

COST ESTIMATE REQUEST

CONTENTS

I. INTRODUCTION

    A. GENERAL
    B. PURPOSE

II. COST ESTIMATE REQUEST FORM
    A. DATE SUBMITTED
    B. DATE REQUIRED
    C. COMPLETION DATE OF ACTUAL WORK
    D. CHARGE TO
    E. TYPE OF ESTIMATE
    F. MANPOWER ESTIMATE
    G. ACCURACY OF ESTIMATE
    H. ESTIMATE REQUIRED BECAUSE
    I. FACTORS KNOWN ABOUT APPLICATION

FIGURE 1: REQUEST FOR COST ESTIMATE

I. INTRODUCTION

A. GENERAL

This practice describes the form to be utilized whenever a cost estimate is required.

B. PURPOSE

This form requires the user to provide information about the nature of the cost estimate request, including the type of estimate required and knowledge of the application.

II. COST ESTIMATE REQUEST FORM

If a user requests a cost estimate, he then completes a Cost Estimate.

Request as shown in Figure 1. This is necessary to avoid confusion about the assumptions on which an estimate is based.

COST ESTIMATE REQUEST	Charge To

COST ESTIMATE REQUEST

Problem Title: _____

Requestor: _____

Dept./Sec.: _____ Ext.: _____

Date Submitted: ____/____/____ Date Required: ____/____/____

The Completion Date of the Actual Work: ____/____/____

Charge To

☐ Overhead

☐ Job No. [____—____] main   sub

If charged to Job No., indicate manhours allowed to prepare estimate ↓

NATURE OF WORK (check one; check which level)

☐ Feasibility Study
☐ New System Development
☐ New System Automation
☐ Complex System Modification
☐ Simple System Modification
☐ Emergency Program Maintenance

☐ Special Study
☐ Other (Describe)

☐ System Level   ☐ Program Level

TYPE OF ESTIMATE (Check one in both areas)

☐ Estimate for Development Costs Only
☐ Estimate for Operational Costs Only
☐ Both

☐ Estimate Direct Costs Only
☐ Estimate Direct & Overhead
☐ External Bid: Estimate Direct, Overhead & Profit

MANPOWER ESTIMATE (to appear as)

☐ Manhours   ☐ Man Weeks (40 hrs.)   ☐ Man Months (168 hrs.)   ☐ Dollars

ACCURACY OF ESTIMATE: ☐ Preliminary   ☐ Approximate   ☐ Accurate

ESTIMATE REQUIRED BECAUSE

☐ External Proposal   ☐ Budget Planning
☐ Internal Proposal   ☐ Budget Allocation
☐ Cost Commitment

☐ Other (justify):

FACTORS KNOWN ABOUT APPLICATION (attach available pertinent documents)

☐ Problem Unknown
☐ Problem defined about _____ %
☐ Preliminary Design Determined
☐ Detailed Design Determined
☐ Program Specs. Available

☐ Other Factors Known:

SPECIAL CONSIDERATIONS (Such as, new equipment, monetary limitations, priority needs, other comments)

Figure 1. Request for cost estimate.

The user should exercise care in completing this form. Allow ample time for an estimate to be properly prepared. Consider the information an analyst will require in order to make a reasonable estimate.

Selected entries on the form are discussed below:

A. DATE SUBMITTED

Submit the Cost Estimate Request as far in advance as possible, to avoid causing backlogs.

B. DATE REQUIRED

Estimates are frequently requested on a rush basis. This time limitation does not allow the person preparing the estimate enough time to determine properly the many factors that go into the estimate. Time requirements should be explained to the user, and a short-span *Date Required* should be avoided where at all possible.

C. COMPLETION DATE OF ACTUAL WORK

The *Completion Date* is filled in by the Requestor, and tells the person preparing the estimate when the services under consideration must be delivered. This information will influence manpower allocations and other factors necessary to an accurate estimate.

D. CHARGE TO

Generally, estimates are charged to overhead. If this is the case, check the block marked *Overhead* and do not fill in the block marked *Job No.*

If the estimate is to be charged to project funds, fill in the block marked *Job No.,* and indicate the manhours allowed to prepare the estimate, for which the project will pay.

E. TYPE OF ESTIMATE

Some users do not distinguish development from operation, but estimates that give a true picture must be based upon the *Type of Estimate.* Check the appropriate block (left side of this entry).

Confusion can arise over whether an estimate includes overhead costs of direct costs only or, in the case of an external bid, if profit is included. Check the appropriate block (right side of this entry).

F. MANPOWER ESTIMATE

A *Manpower Estimate* is needed in many cases. It may be expressed as manhours, man-weeks, or man-months (for large developments). The conversion factor for hours-to-weeks-to-months should be standard within the company (as indicated in this area of the form). If a manpower estimate is desired in units of time, check the block indicating how it is to appear.

A *Manpower Estimate* in terms of dollars may be desired. If this is the case, check the block marked "Dollars." It should be realized that dollar estimates require knowledge of the latest salary level for each required labor category.

G. ACCURACY OF ESTIMATE

The degree of accuracy the Requestor needs is based upon how the estimate is to be used. A manager may wish only a preliminary idea of how much an ADP system will cost; a response that it will cost $40,000 to $50,000 would be sufficient. Or, he may wish to pinpoint it between $2,000 and $3,000, or within a leeway of 10%. If the estimate is for an outside bid, it must be extremely accurate to be competitive, yet show a profit.

H. ESTIMATE REQUIRED BECAUSE

The Requestor should identify the reason for the estimate being required, since the degree of accuracy of the estimate is related to it.

If the reason the estimate is required is one of the listed reasons, check the appropriate block. If it does not fall within one of the categories shown, check the block marked "Other," indicate the reason, and justify it.

I. FACTORS KNOWN ABOUT APPLICATION

Any special considerations that affect the estimate, such as the purchase of new hardware devices, monetary limitations, priority needs, or other considerations, should be set forth here. Examples of special comments might be: "Consider the use of OCR equipment as the data input medium;" "One hard copy device is needed for each cluster of four terminals. The terminals must have keyboard editing features to facilitate test editing applications."

PRACTICE 0130
FEASIBILITY STUDY

CONTENTS

I.   INTRODUCTION

    A. GENERAL
    B. PURPOSE

II. STUDY CONTENT

III. PRESENTATION OF RESULTS

I. INTRODUCTION

A. GENERAL

This practice describes the function and content of the feasibility study that shall be performed for all new development projects or major revisions to existing systems.

B. PURPOSE

This practice provides an outline, or table of contents, of the feasibility study, and a brief explanation of the kinds of information to be contained in each point of the outline.

II. STUDY CONTENT

The goal of the feasibility study is to provide decision-makers with the information they need to determine the advisability of proceeding with system development. The content of the feasibility study will vary from project to project, depending on the scope of the undertaking.

For a project involving a large capital outlay, a thorough risk analysis should be performed. For instance, a company may be considering distributive processing as a means of providing greater local control as well as dollar savings. The vendors of distributive processing hardware and software are unlikely to reveal the lack of interface development between the central system, the communication network, and the local nodes. For example, one national corporation ended up having to use four different vendors to put a system together. The minicomputer vendor did not have a satisfactory terminal. Differences in protocol required the use of a piece of hardware which was only available through another vendor. The point is that a good feasibility study would have isolated the risks that were glossed over in the all-glowing presentation of the new project.

The bottom line of a good feasibility study is the honest statement of the positive and negative sides of the project under consideration. The finding of difficulties in the project plan does not mean that approval will be withheld.

Catch-22 of a feasibility study is that extensive preliminary digging is required to identify the risks and benefits of a project. Customers object to spending the money on a project without having a go-ahead. In our earlier example, the system development staff did not realize the number of interface problems that would be encountered.

There is no formula for how much preliminary mapping out of the project is needed. The general guide is the more novel the approach, the more digging is needed. Thus, in introducing a novel system, it is essential to lay it out in advance, and fully describe all technical problems which must be worked out in the design.

While it is easy to discuss the positive reasons for supporting a project, it is usually difficult in a feasibility study to support your rationale with factual information. For instance, projected cost savings or contributions to company success are uncertain before the study is completed. The most solid approach is to identify, point by point, the problems of the way the work is presently being performed. For example, in the current system, 20% of the orders may be rejected because of errors. The productivity of the data entry staff may be far below what has been reported by other organizations. In the feasibility study, then, precise descriptions should be given of how the proposed system will be superior to the current one; e.g., if you are predicting that there will be a ninety percent reduction in error rate, describe how it will be brought about. For instance, you may be proposing to establish a distributed system for order entry in which the people who write the orders will enter them into the computer. Can you back up your contentions with citations of companies which have achieved the results that you anticipate with a similar system design? *The more factual you are, the more weight the feasibility study will carry.* In the feasibility study, you want to get at the realistic considerations that need answers, in order to properly evaluate merits of a project.

1. **WHAT WILL HAPPEN TO EMPLOYEES WHO OPERATE THE EXISTING SYSTEM?**

As an example, if the orders are currently being prepared at the central computer site, does this mean that sixty percent of the employees will have to be let go? Will any of them be needed at dispersed sites under the new system? Are the projected cost savings realistic in the environment of the computer? If the number of employees is to remain the same, then the savings will come as the company expands, without having to add new clerical personnel.

2. WHAT ARE THE ALTERNATIVE APPROACHES TO SOLVING THE INFORMATION PROBLEM?

If a thorough examination were made of all major alternatives, the cost of a feasibility study would be out of proportion to total project costs. If only one approach is really being considered, it does not make much sense to describe all the other approaches and then throw them out as unworkable. For example, a study of word processing requirements would not consider stand-alone word processing typewriters, if minicomputers were needed to meet the application requirements. Where there are several viable alternatives, it then becomes worthwhile to consider the costs and benefits of each in the feasibility study.

3. HOW WILL THE NEW SYSTEM WORK?

A description of how the new system will work is often left out of a feasibility study. But if you cannot explain how it will work, management really is not able to appreciate why you are planning to install it. For example, minicomputers in the branch banks will be used to handle accounting functions and reduce the number of back-room personnel. To make it understandable you would have to explain how the computer will be used for daily proofing of account transactions, and how information will be integrated with the overall bank management information system.

4. WHAT IS THE SYSTEM DEVELOPMENT WORK PLAN?

This is another difficult area because to have a complete development area you must have looked at all the detailed steps required. But a feasibility study is wanted by the users at the initial stages of the project. If the project is not planned out enough to lay out a milestone chart with some degree of reliability, then you may consider describing on a phase basis the most important tasks to be done; e.g., finding a terminal that has the features needed, developing an interface between the terminal and the central computer, etc.

5. WHAT ARE THE PLANS FOR CONVERTING THE DATA BASE?

This is an area which is omitted from many feasibility studies, but turns out to be one of the most important aspects of the project. For example, a company may be planning to develop an integrated data base for financial applications. One of the largest tasks of the project will be to standardize the format and method of calculation. Data conversion will involve a number of user groups to work together to agree to standardize formats, and then to laboriously convert the data.

6.   WHAT ARE THE PLANS FOR TESTING THE SYSTEM OUT?

Managers who must approve a project, and who have experience with previous ADP systems, are aware of the difficulties of obtaining an operationally reliable system.   While it is unconventional to have a feasibility study delve into a phase of work which takes place after the system has already been designed, it should be dealt with whenever you have a major project. Psychologically, the inclusion of a section on this topic will impress the reviewers with the thoroughness of the plan.

III.   PRESENTATION OF RESULTS

The essential problem with feasibility studies getting a fair hearing is that people who are judging the project merits are the people who are apt to be the busiest. Therefore, the findings must be forceful and to the point.   What you are trying to do is to have the reader see how you reached your conclusion so that he can see how well you conceptualized the problem.   Some feasibility studies go overboard in microscopic analysis of the current system, and others make glib generalizations unsubstantiated by empirical evidence. If there is too much detail, the manager will not have enough time to sort out the major factors that come into play in making the decision. Glibness leaves the reader with an uneasy feeling that this proposed project may not have been well thought out. A standard approach is to write a management summary that highlights the findings and recommendations. This works well when directed to an executive who does not wish to be involved in the project.

An approach that is highly effective is to make definitive statements of the conclusions, and then to support them. Examples are:

"Maintenance will be a problem in our Western offices. None of the chosen minicomputer vendors have a readily available staff for maintenance in low-population density locations."

Support: We can train our own personnel to replace components, but down time will be considerably higher than at the central site. Savings of $300,000 will be realized in the second year of operation if we amortize development costs over ten years. Reason: Automatic reorder of retail grocery items will enable us to reduce our retail inventory by 20%. The interest savings on the capital that we will no longer require is the source of the above savings. Because of the cost of maintaining a parallel system, there will be an anticipated $200,000 loss the first year.

"The online data entry using a distributed system design is the most cost-effective."

Support: The communications costs of a centralized online approach make the transactions costs far in excess of what can be tolerated; 80¢ per order versus 40¢ per order in the recommended alternative. Seventy percent of errors are content incompatabilities. Most could be corrected as the data is entered, eliminating the wasted effort of recycling the input records under a batch approach.

Initially, it is intimidating to use this format, since you may not have solid evidence for the statements you make. You must have the attitude of a trial attorney who presents all the evidence he has to support his contentions. He knows that some may be debatable. Yet he is willing to go out on a limb because he has confidence in the overall arguments he is presenting.

IDENTIFICATION STANDARDS

CONTENTS

I. INTRODUCTION

    A. GENERAL
    B. PURPOSE

II. JOB CONTROL LANGUAGE
    CONVENTIONS

FIGURE 1: NAMING CONVENTIONS

I. INTRODUCTION

A. GENERAL

This practice describes a set of simple naming conventions that facilitate the interpretation of all documentation associated with the system.

B. PURPOSE

This standard contains an explicit set of naming conventions which are to be used in all development and operations documentation of the system.

II. JOB CONTROL LANGUAGE CONVENTIONS

A. NAMING CONVENTIONS

In the context of the data processing environment, a properly structured name becomes a very important element of information. A structured name may identify a customer, application program, type of job processed, or any other similar information. Such names, or identifiers, should be kept simple and flexible. Complexity in such items can often defeat their usefulness. With these fundamentals in mind, unique identifiers have been structured for:

1. System names
2. Timesharing system initials
3. Job names
4. Programmer name
5. Catalogued procedure names
6. Application program names
7. Step names
8. Data set names
9. Line printer report names

Specific rules and conventions for these names have been summarized for easy reference in Figure 1.

NAMING CONVENTIONS

Code	Purpose	Convention
System Name	Identifies a specific production system.	A two-character alpha code.
Timesharing system Initials	Identifies a particular facility to be used.	Three characters specified by computer operations.
Job Name	Identifies a particular jobstream or job within a given production system.	A concatenation of the WYLBUR initials and the system name.
Function ID	A parameter on the job card used to identify the job and system.	Twenty characters of information which briefly describes the function of the job and the frequency. Examples might be: 'PAYROLL MAST EDIT-DLY' or 'WKLY ACCTS AUDIT.'
Catalogued Procedure name	Identifies unique procedures with various production systems.	An eight-character code consisting of: aaPROCbb, where: a=System Name PROC=CONSTANT b=Sequence Number
Program Name	Identifies a particular program within a given system.	A seven-character code: aabccdd, where: a=System Name b=Language A=ALC C=COBOL F=Fortran I=Inquire P=PL/I

Figure 1. Naming conventions.

Code	Purpose	Convention
		U=Utility X=Special c=General Function of the Program ED=Edit FM=File Maintenance RE=Report QY=All-purpose query RV=Recovery Program UT=Utility XX=Other d=Sequence Number (01,02,...)
Step Name	Identifies unique steps within a given procedure.	Eight characters of information of the form aaxxx,xxx. where: a=System Code x=Free form (EDIT3, PRT2, etc.)
Data Set Name	Identifies and describes production system data sets.	A maximum of 44 characters with the following format: CNaaaa.iii.bb.cccccccc.dddd Where: CNaaa.iii=Fixed by OSI b=System Name c=Description (variable) d=Type of data set MAST=Master file HIST=History file TRAN=Transaction file WORK=Work file SLIB=Source Library LLIB=Load Library PROC=Procedure Library UTIL=Utility file SPEC=Special or other REPT=Report file
Line Printer Report Name	Uniquely identify all line printer reports.	A concatenation of the seven-character program name that produced the report and a sequence number for those programs

Figure 1. (*continued*)

Code	Purpose	Convention
		producing more than one report. aaaaaaa-bb Where: a=Program Name '–'=Constant b=Sequence Number (01,02, etc.)

Figure 1. (*continued*)

PRACTICE 0150

COST-BENEFIT ANALYSIS GUIDELINE

CONTENTS

I. INTRODUCTION

    A. GENERAL
    B. PURPOSE

II. PERSONNEL-RELATED COSTS

III. COMPUTER-RELATED COSTS

    A. TAB, EAM, AND KEYPUNCH
    B. TERMINALS AND COMMUNICATIONS
    C. HARDWARE REMOVAL OR ADDITION

IV. PROCESSING COSTS

V. REVENUE-RELATED COSTS

VI. OTHER COSTS

VII. COST CHANGES OVER TIME

VIII. OVERALL BENEFITS

    A. TYPES OF DIRECT BENEFITS
    B. TYPES OF BENEFITS DEPENDENT
       UPON SYSTEM USES

XI. TIME-PHASED RETURN ON
     INVESTMENT

   A. OPERATING COSTS
   B. OTHER BENEFITS
   C. DEVELOPMENT COSTS
   D. WORST CASE ANALYSIS

FIGURE 1: CPU USAGE FORM
FIGURE 2: SUMMARY OF COSTS, BENEFITS,
           AND NET PRESENT VALUE
FIGURE 3: DEVELOPMENT COST

I. INTRODUCTION

A. GENERAL

The operating cost-benefit analysis demonstrates the "steady-state" improvement that the new system will cause *relative* to the cost of continuing to operate the current system.   The review of current systems has carefully laid out the current system operations costs. Now these operating costs must be estimated for the new or modified system.

B. PURPOSE

This practice provides some guidelines and forms for estimating costs and benefits of the new system.

II. PERSONNEL-RELATED COSTS

Personnel utilization should be determined during the review of the current system.   Each area should then be examined in view of the new design, and any personnel savings estimated.   Any new personnel required by the new system should be figured into the cost analysis.   Estimates should be conservative; i.e., 2.4 people should be rounded to 2 in the case of a reduction, and to 3 in the case of an addition.   Personnel estimates should not be reduced linearly with reduced manual workload because it is usually the more difficult and/or time-consuming tasks that the computer cannot handle. Possible reduction factors are:

% Manual Workload Reduction	% Personnel Reduction
100	100
90	75
80	65
70	50
60	35
50	25
40	20
30	15
20	0

Each specific area of cost reduction should be detailed in the text of the analysis. For personnel cost, full salaries as well as overhead expenses should be used.

These estimated savings (or additional costs) must be reviewed with the user departments for agreement. Without concurrence, the analysis is going to be met with heavy opposition.

III. COMPUTER-RELATED COSTS

It is important to consider the total impact of computer-related costs in the cost-benefit analysis, rather than any individual savings. It is quite possible that the implementation of an online data entry facility might allow the removal of a dedicated small computer in the field, but this savings may be more than offset by the increased processing costs at the central site. Only the overall impact is meaningful.

Hardware related costs are those associated with the replacement, removal, or purchase of dedicated computer-related hardware, equipment, communications lines, etc. The entire cost of a new computer to be dedicated to a system must be counted as a cost against the project. Shared resources, such as a high-capacity computer, which processes non-system-related work, must be costed to their users. These are considered under Section IV (Processing Costs).

A. TAB, EAM, AND KEYPUNCH

Any tabulating, electrical accounting machine (EAM), or keypunch equipment, removed or added as a result of the implementation of a new system, must be accounted for as dedicated costs. If fully paid equipment is removed, no cost-benefit should be claimed unless the equipment has a salvage value. The monthly rental cost for equipment, had it not been purchased, is irrelevant to an estimator.

B. TERMINALS AND COMMUNICATIONS

Any expected additional costs or savings of data entry terminals (e.g., CRT inquiry terminals), communications lines costs (e.g., WATS lines), and other *dedicated* communications-related hardware (e.g., concentrators, controllers, front-end) must be included in the analysis.

C.   HARDWARE REMOVAL OR ADDITION

The removal or addition of *dedicated* equipment must be specified. Purchased equipment is a one-time cost, but for cost-benefit analysis it should be amortized over its useful life or the life of the system.

IV.   PROCESSING COSTS

Ideally, any resource which is shared between more than one system, should have its cost allocated in proportion to the using systems. In fact, the computer is the main place where this occurs, although communications costs are also sometimes broken down this way. For communications costs allocations, the fraction of total network usage by each system is calculated.

Processing costs can best be estimated by determining the fraction of computer use by the new system. There are two basic approaches to this:

- Knowing the total usage and the potential using systems usage, and then fractionally allocating.
- Assuming what the total usage will be, and then fractionally allocating.

In practice, especially for large systems, the second approach is more feasible.

Defining a measure of computer usage is necessary, in order to allocate costs properly. One way to do this is to regard the processing unit (CPU) as the central resource, and to allocate all computer costs (peripheral, operators, etc.) on the basis of the CPU utilization. If there is a significant exception to this algorithm (i.e., an additional cost of the new system that will not be reflected in the CPU-based estimates), the additional cost can be added to the estimates.

By counting the number of physical I/O's (not READs or WRITEs), data base logical I/O's and the number of transactions to be processed per run, the CPU utilization of the new system can be calculated if the CPU utilization per transaction is known. Tables, such as those below, and the form in Figure 1 can be used for the calculation (note that run frequency and machine configuration must be known).

Of course, it is difficult to know the number of transactions that will be processed. Different type transactions will require fewer or more I/O's, and we may not know how many of each will occur. Estimates here again should be conservative. You might show the worst and average case.

I/O CPU TIMES (msec), COBOL assumed

| | | MACHINE | | | |
		370/155	370/158	370/165	370/168
	Sequential	0.50	0.40	0.25	0.20
	Direct	2.00	1.40	0.80	0.60
I/O	ISAM	4.00	2.60	1.40	1.00
	Data Base	15.00	11.00	7.00	4.50

PROCESS CPU TIMES (msec/txn)

| | | MACHINE | | | |
		370/155	370/158	370/165	370/168
	Simple	4.00	3.00	1.75	1.10
COMPLEXITY	Average	10.00	8.00	4.75	2.75
	Difficult	20.00	15.00	8.75	5.50

V. REVENUE-RELATED COSTS

Savings or costs that relate to a change in the cash position of the firm must be considered. For example, if the new system provides a more efficient billing system, resulting in funds being received sooner, this will have a positive impact on the financial position of the firm. The value of receiving money earlier may be calculated.

VI. OTHER ITEMS

Any other miscellaneous costs or savings should also be recognized. Examples of costs might include the purchase of software, or start-up costs, or cost associated with winning acceptance by unions, consumer groups, etc.

VII. COST CHANGES OVER TIME

Costs do not remain constant over time. In addition to general inflation, relative costs change (e.g., the cost per man-hour has increased greatly in relation to the cost of the average computer resource unit in the last several years). Trends may be anticipated: (1) cost will flatten out as inflation is brought under control, (2) productivity gains will be the main justification for new computer systems, and (3) computer processing costs will not decline at the last five-year rate and may even go up. As far as possible, when estimating development and operating costs for future years, costing should be based on expected trends.

VIII. OVERALL BENEFITS

Benefits from systems can be divided into two general types:
- Direct—due directly to the system
- Dependent on Use of the System, resulting from secondary or indirect effects.

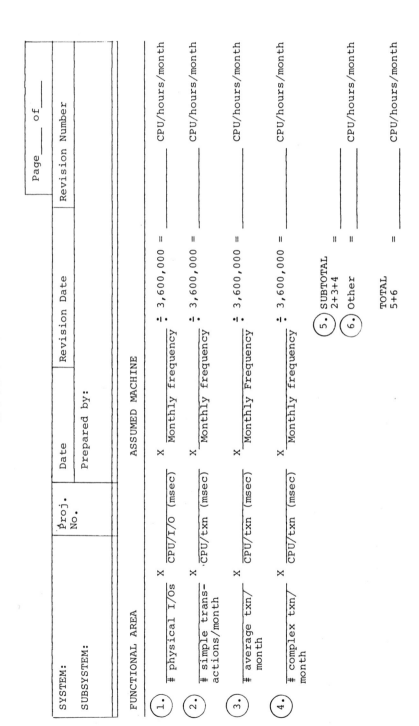

Figure 1. CPU utilization form.

A. **DIRECT BENEFITS**

1. *Administrative Cost Reduction*

Direct benefits result when a system performs work formerly handled manually at less cost (e.g., a system which eliminates several employees performing a filing process).

Of course, the new system will probably require its own manpower (operators, technicians, etc.) and therefore the net effect must be considered. The management responsible for implementing the change should determine what manpower will be required with the new system.

2. *Efficiency Improvement*

More direct benefits accrue when the system causes productivity to rise. Specifics of each situation will determine the unit of measurement. Care should be taken to insure that the potential reductions are not just that. Will the workers be required to take on new duties or just have more time to dawdle?

3. *Improved Operations and Controls*

If the new system results in increased management control, the value of this control is a direct benefit. To measure such benefits, the management of the associated operation must make the estimate, considering that there are often uncertainties about the amount of the potential savings. How will this increased control turn into dollars?

4. *One-time Savings*

Implementation of a system could lead to a one-time saving, such as a reduction in the need to expand present plant may be blunted by more efficient utilization of the current plant.

5. *New Business Revenues*

It is often overlooked that a new system will in itself contribute to increased sales. Many new services today are computer based. Portable terminals are now being used to take customer restaurant orders. Order taking is much faster. Orders are flashed to the proper cooking station right from the customer location.

B. **INDIRECT BENEFITS**

1. *Management Process*

The management method of a firm may be affected by the new system. Planning, control, resource allocation, etc. may be changed by the implementation of a new system. Measuring the benefits derived here is difficult, however. The system analysis should include a list of the potential changes and a qualitative assessment of the results.

2. *Better Information*

A new system may provide information not previously available. The information could be instrumental in the decision making process and result in increased profitability in a variety of ways. Without a job cost and profitability system, a firm only knows aggregate costs and profitability. The new system could provide the ability to price products so that a predetermined profit margin is achieved at all items. Store managers will be able to concentrate on profitable items and drop less profitable ones. If an estimate of the volume of goods sold needed to break even is made, and then the average profitability of the firm is substituted for the zero profit level, you can then measure the increase in profitability by changing the mix of items being sold, without a change in volume.

3. *Improved Service or Product*

A new system may enable a firm to provide new products or services to its customers. The benefits of such a system must be measured in the same manner as any other product or service change. How much more will people pay for this new capability? Will more people use it?

4. *Longer-term outcomes*

Systems may result in long-term benefits that are difficult to quantify:
- Increased flexibility of management action—implementing a general inventory system allows management to rapidly make changes in the firm's inventory records, which would be more difficult with a manual system.
- Ability to expand in the face of increasing volume—A new system could be designed that is able to handle increased production.
- Ability to handle additional functions—A new system may have abilities the old one did not, which benefit related areas of the firm. For example, a new payroll system may have a master employee file that can be used by the personnel administration office as well. It will facilitate evolving into a full data base environment.

The benefits above are difficult to measure quantitatively. Also, they may be misleading. You may justify a new computer based on its ability to handle expanded volume, but may end up with unwanted overhead. In the system analysis, the features and capabilities in terms of future utilization should be clearly

SYSTEM:	Proj. No.	Date	Revision Date	Revision Number	Page ___ of ___
SUBSYSTEM:		Prepared by:			

	TIME PERIOD								TOTALS
1. Proposed system operating cost									
2. Existing system operating cost									
3. Incremental operating cost (2 minus 1)									
4. Other Benefits									
5. Total cash benefits (3 plus 4)									
6. Development cost									
7. Net costs (5 minus 6)									
8. Discount factors									
9. Discounted cash flow (7 times 8)									

NET PRESENT VALUE

ASSUMPTIONS: Discount rate + ____ %
Number of years to pay back development costs before taxes ____

Figure 2. Summary of costs, benefits, and net present value.

identified and fully explained, so that they may be weighed as accurately as possible against the costs.

IX. TIME-PHASED RETURN ON INVESTMENT

The net present value of a system must be determined to make realistic judgements about its worth. A future gain may be larger than an immediate gain, but when discounted to its present value it could be smaller. A format such as shown in Figure 2 should be used to convert the various parameters.

A. OPERATING COSTS

Operating costs of both the present system and the proposed system should be calculated at the expected prices for each year of the expected life of the system from implementation (5-10 years). Three factors are important in these computations:

- The size of the business in terms of the number of transactions, locations, etc. Known or anticipated changes should also be considered.
- Price level changes, including inflation factors, improved technology in related fields resulting in lower costs, etc.
- Timing of the changes involved in the new system, such as staff reduction or need for additional office space.

B. DEVELOPMENT COSTS

Figure 3 provides the development costs by time period, and the results should be entered into Figure 2. Instructions for filling in the form are as follows:

1. *Development Cost by Phase*

The first table demonstrates the development cost by phase and resource type.

2. *Description*

The description of the resource type, such as analyst, manager, computer time, hardware, etc.

3. *Code*

The code assigned to this type of resource.

4. *Cost*

The cost per resource unit is noted here.

5. *Units*

DEVELOPMENT COST

PART I

Page ______ of ______

SYSTEM:	Proj No.	Date	Rev. Date	Rev. No.
SUBSYSTEM:	Prepared by:			

RESOURCE TYPE			DEVELOPMENT COST BY PHASE (1)											
			Phase I (7)		Phase IIA		Phase IIB		Phase III		Phase IV		Total	
Description	Code	Cost	Units	$	Units	$	Units	$	Units	$	Units	$	Units	$
(2)	(3)	(4)	(5)	(6)										
TOTAL														

Figure 3. Development cost.

DEVELOPMENT COST

PART II

| SYSTEM | | Proj. No. | Date | Rev. Date | Page ___ of ___ |
| SUBSYSTEM: | | Prepared By: | | | Rev. No. |

DEVELOPMENT COST OVER TIME (BY PERIOD) ⑧

RESOURCE TYPE			⑨													
Description	Code	Cost	Units	$	Units	$	Units	$	Units	$	Units	$	Units	$	Units	$
	⑩	⑪														
TOTAL																

Figure 3. (*continued*)

The units of the resource requirements must be put here. This may be different units for different resources, such as days for personnel, hours of computer itme, or number of trips for travel costs. This information can be derived by summing end resource type by phase.

6. *Cost*

This is the product of 4 and 5 above.

7. *Phase*

Each phase is listed separately on this table.

8. *Cost by Time Period*

This table spreads the costs over the development time period as the previous table spreads the costs over the development cycle.

9. *Time Period*

The time period used here should be the same as the one used on the milestone plan.

10. *Units*

The abbreviation for the resource unit is entered here.

11. *Cost*

The cost is derived the same as in the previous chart, Numbers 1 through 7 above.

The resulting net costs per year must be discounted back to present dollars (or to the assumed date of initial implementation). The discount rate to be used depends on the management's cut-off rate for investments, and is related to the firm's cost of obtaining capital.

Net present value factors at 10% are:

	Present	*6 months in future*
Current Year (Year 0)	1	.909
Year 1	.909	.823
Year 2	.826	.746
Year 3	.751	.677
Year 4	.683	.614
Year 5	.621	.557
Year 6	.546	.505
Year 7	.513	.458
Year 8	.467	.405
Year 9	.424	.377
Year 10	.386	.342

The year used should depend on the expected life of the system, once it is implemented, usually 5-7 years.

D. WORST CASE ANALYSIS

In keeping with our emphasis on conservative estimating, the same calculations above should be made based on the "worst case" assumptions. These could include:

- An additional year of development time
- 50% more money necessary for development or implementation
- 50% higher operating costs
- 50% lower revenue availability benefit.

PRACTICE 0160

HARDWARE RESOURCE REQUIREMENTS ESTIMATE

CONTENTS

I. INTRODUCTION

    A. GENERAL
    B. PURPOSE

II. HARDWARE ANALYSIS FORMS

    A. HARDWARE ANALYSIS
    B. RESOURCE REQUIREMENTS ESTIMATE
    C. PHYSICAL HARDWARE REQUIREMENTS
        ESTIMATE
    D. ESTABLISH SURPLUS OR DEFICIENCY
        OF HARDWARE
    E. TECHNICAL SUPPORT REVIEW
    F. TRAINING

FIGURE 1: AVAILABLE HARDWARE
           ENVIRONMENT
FIGURE 2: ESTIMATED HARDWARE USAGE
FIGURE 3: RESOURCE REQUIREMENTS
           TRANSACTION FORM
FIGURE 4: EXPECTED HARDWARE DEFICIENCY
           OR SURPLUS
FIGURE 5: HARDWARE ISSUES TO BE
           CONSIDERED

INTRODUCTION

A. GENERAL

This practice outlines the basic steps for calculating hardware resource requirements that a new system will require. Included is a set of forms which allow the planning of hardware requirements for a period of up to 24 months.

B. PURPOSE

This practice provides a means of analyzing hardware resource requirements in sufficient detail to plan future installations.

AVAILABLE HARDWARE ENVIRONMENT

			Page _____ of _____				
SYSTEM:			Date	Rev. Date	Rev. No.		
SUBSYSTEM:			Prepared by:				
AVAILABLE SYSTEM COMPONENTS	Indicate Availability in Units of:	Date __/__/__ Currently Available	+6 Months	+12 Months	+18 Months	+24 Months	
CPU (Model____)	%						
Main memory	kilobytes						
Tapes (Model____)	≠ of Drives						
Discs (Model ____)	≠ of Packs						
Communication Lines (____speed)	Number of Lines						
Terminals pe ____)	Number						

Figure 1. Available hardware environment.

II. HARDWARE ANALYSIS FORMS

A. HARDWARE AVAILABLE

In analyzing the hardware picture, what first must be determined is the available capacity. The form shown in Figure 1 may be used for compiling this information. Under consideration are the following concepts:

- Hardware components time-phased availability; that is, considering hardware on order, on-site, scheduled delivery dates, manufacturer's lead time, etc.
- The available hardware components for this specific application; that is, considering present systems which will be still in operation and proposed systems estimated resource requirements

A baseline for comparison with a similar projection of new system needs is provided by completing the forms shown in Figures 2, 3, and 4.

A listing of hardware resources is provided in Figure 1. The specific installation's model numbers should be entered. If they are crucial to this application, additional resources or sub-components of entered resources may be added. Intervals of six months comprise the time frame. Consideration of this allows for lead times for manufacture or installation, and ordering and approval delays.

The indicated measure of the resource under consideration should be entered. To illustrate, the availability of CPU is entered as a percentage of the indicated CPU model. The number of packs of the specific type that can be online at one time indicates disk availability. Also to be considered are purchase decisions which have been made.

B. RESOURCE REQUIREMENTS ESTIMATE

Resource estimates are considered in Figure 2, and are listed in units closest to the design specification. For example, rather than expressing CPU requirements as a percent of CPU, they would be listed in hours. Likewise, rather than expressing disk requirements as the number of packs, they would be listed as the number of bytes. Also listed should be the largest simultaneous need for resources; for example, communication lines, disks and tapes. Rather than entering the number of devices of percentages, enter units of resource measurement in the hardware usage plan to account for the many factors in relating these requirements to actual hardware needs.

C. PHYSICAL HARDWARE REQUIREMENTS ESTIMATE

The multi-part form shown in Figure 3 is used for translating the new system's resource requirements into actual hardware requirements. All factors that affect actual device utilization may be entered. For example, such factors as maximum actual CPU utilization and average up-time are taken into account in arriving at percentage CPU utilization

ESTIMATED HARDWARE USAGE

		Page _____ of _____			
SYSTEM:		Date	Revision Date	Revision No.	
SUBSYSTEM:		Prepared by:			
REQUIRED SYSTEM COMPONENTS	Indicate Requirements in Units of:	Date __/__/__	+6 Months	+12 Months	+18 Months	+24 Months
CPU (Model _____)	Hours/Months					
Main Memory	Kilobytes					
Tapes (Model ___)	Total Drive hours/day					
	Largest simultaneous number of drives					
Discs (Model ___)	Kilobytes on-line					
	Largest simultaneous number of drives					
Communications lines	Total bytes Day					
	Largest bytes/ hour rate					
Terminals (Type___)	Number					

Figure 2. Estimated hardware usage.

from the number of CPU hours needed. Wasted space and blocking efficiency are two factors taken into account in arriving at the number of disk packs required. Considering these factors contributes to a more precise statement of device requirements.

D. ESTABLISH SURPLUS OR DEFICIENCY OF HARDWARE

When the numbers in Figure 3 are subtracted from those in Figure 1,

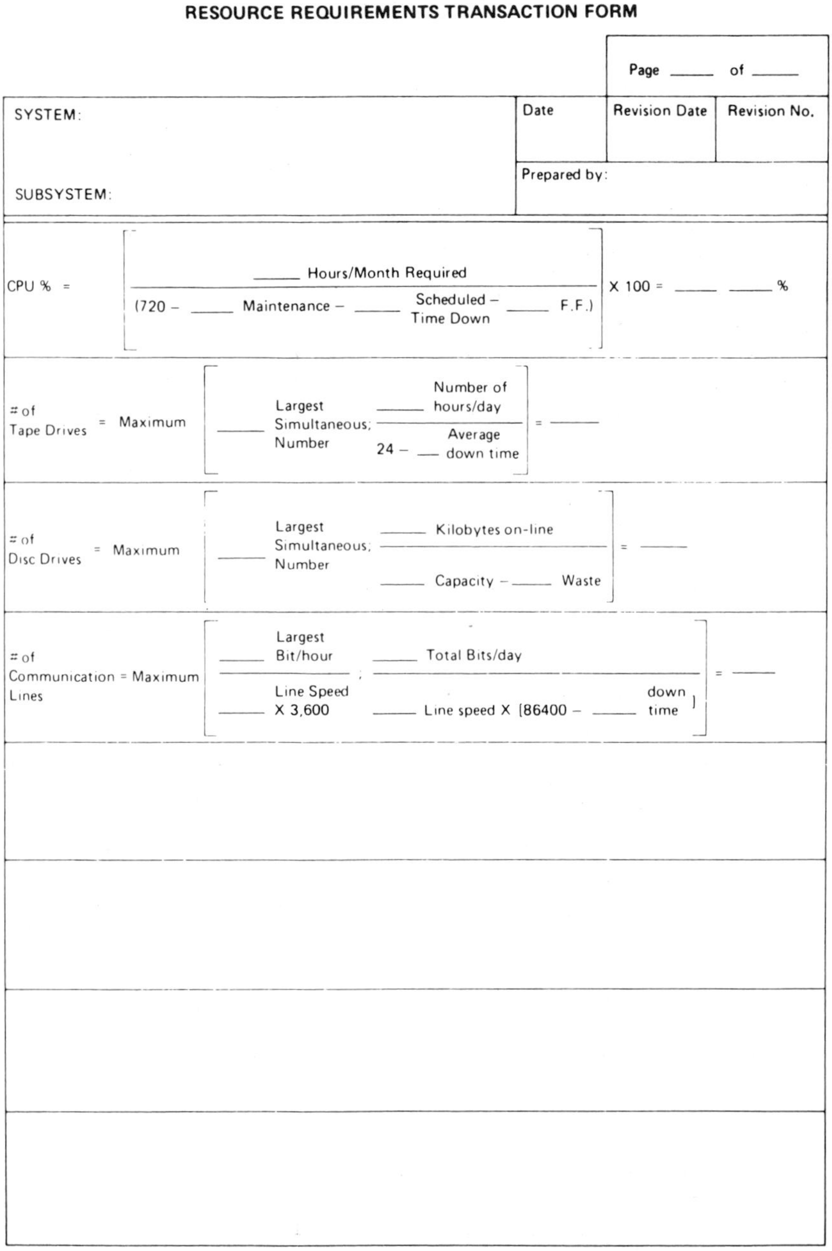

RESOURCE REQUIREMENTS TRANSACTION FORM

Page ____ of ____

SYSTEM:	Date	Revision Date	Revision No.
SUBSYSTEM:	Prepared by:		

CPU % = [____ Hours/Month Required / (720 − ____ Maintenance − ____ Scheduled − Time Down ____ F.F.)] X 100 = ____ ____ %

# of Tape Drives = Maximum [____ Largest Simultaneous; Number ____ Number of hours/day / 24 − ____ Average down time] = ____

# of Disc Drives = Maximum [____ Largest Simultaneous; Number ____ Kilobytes on-line / ____ Capacity − ____ Waste] = ____

# of Communication Lines = Maximum [____ Largest Bit/hour / ____ Line Speed X 3,600 ; ____ Total Bits/day / ____ Line speed X (86400 − ____ down time)] = ____

Figure 3. Resource requirements transaction form.

the difference is entered in Figure 4. Excess capacity is expressed in positive numbers, while hardware deficiency is expressed in negative numbers. All negative numbers should be reentered in Figure 5, because of the need to analyze hardware deficiency. The factors that should be considered are the device in question, the date of the first projected deficiency, and the projected amount of the deficiency.

Comments about the deficiency, and the methods of solution, should be entered by the analyst. A check mark in the last column should be used to note specific problems, such as equipment with long manufacturer' lead time. By using this form as a management guide, individuals can be assigned to tackle specific problems.

EXPECTED HARDWARE DEFICIENCY OR SURPLUS

				Page _____ of _____		
SYSTEM:			Date	Revision Date	Revision No.	
SUBSYSTEM:			Prepared by:			
AVAILABLE SYSTEM COMPONENTS	Indicate Availability in Units of	DATE __ /__ /__ Currently Available	+6 Months	+12 Months	+18 Months	+24 Months
CPU (Model___)	%					
Main memory	kilobytes					
Tapes (Model___)	# of Drives					
Discs (Model___)	# of Packs					
Communication Lines ____ speed)	Number of Lines					
Terminals (Type ___)	Number					

Figure 4. Expected hardware deficiency or surplus.

HARDWARE ISSUES TO BE CONSIDERED

SYSTEM				Date	Rev. Date	Rev. No.
				Prepared by:		
SUBSYSTEM:						
DEVICE	DATE OF FIRST EXPECTED DEFICIENCY	EXPECTED AMOUNT OF DEFICIENCY	COMMENTS (Reasons, Lead Times, etc.)			REQUIRE IMMEDIATE ATTENTION (OR DATE)
1.						
2.						
3.						
4.						
5.						
6.						
7.						
8.						
9.						
10.						
11.						
12.						
13.						
14.						
15.						
16.						

Figure 5. Hardware issues to be considered.

E. TECHNICAL SUPPORT REVIEW

The technical support group normally analyzes the hardware environment. Figure 2 would typically be completed by the project analyst, and then forwarded to the technical support analyst. A joint presentation to management should be made after the two analysts have conferred.

F. TRAINING

In determining the environment for a system development project, some factors which should be considered are the availability of personnel for development and the overall training picture. For example, training is a more important consideration if only entry-level people can be hired, rather than experienced people. In this analysis, the time-phased development plan is a key factor.

SERIES 0200
system development

PRACTICE 0210

STRUCTURED DEVELOPMENT METHODOLOGY GUIDELINE

CONTENTS

I. INTRODUCTION

    A. GENERAL
    B. PURPOSE

II. STRUCTURED DESIGN PRINCIPLES

III. STRUCTURED DESIGN REVIEWS

    A. REVIEW METHODOLOGY
    B. REQUIREMENTS DEFINITION REVIEW
    C. GENERAL DESIGN REVIEW
    D. DETAIL DESIGN REVIEW
    E. PROGRAMMING REVIEW
    F. OPERATING INSTRUCTIONS REVIEW

    FIGURE 1: STRUCTURE CHART FOR A
                 PERSONNEL DATA ENTRY SYSTEM

    FIGURE 2: A SCHEMATIC DIAGRAM OF THE
                 FACTORING OF INFORMATION FLOW

I. INTRODUCTION

A. GENERAL

This practice describes the basic principles of structured design and the rationale for using this approach to replace conventional design approaches. It also discusses the review process that goes hand-in-hand with the structured development procedure.

It digresses from the other practices in that it is more a philosophy than a detail procedure. Unless the philosophy is accepted by management and a real commitment made to it, it will have no meaningful impact. There must be a unified approach in design, program constriction and documentation.

The Hierarchy plus Input-Process Output (HIPO) documentation technique described in the short HIPO Documentation Guideline practice provides documentation highly suitable to the review process that is described in this practice.

B. PURPOSE

This practice describes the principles of structured design and the procedures for reviewing the design as it progresses through the various developmental stages.

II. STRUCTURED DESIGN PRINCIPLES

Structured design is a methodology for designing systems. It is the art of designing components in the best possible way. However, design is still an *art*. To date no methodology has been developed which will render sound, efficiently designed systems from raw requirements. This guide is a summarized version of structured design which seeks to provide the analyst with two basic tools—a structured chart and a data flow diagram. The aim of these guidelines is to provide assistance during the earliest stages of system design to aid the analyst in "thinking through" the problem.

The underpinnings of structured design are rigorous, sophisticated mathematical relationships. This overview should then serve only as a general guide. For most it will prove more than sufficient.

The objective of structured design is to design a system which seeks the best solution within established terms, within recognized limitations, and within necessary compromises imposed by the "real world." It seeks to design systems which are:

- *Reliable*—have a high mean-time-between-failure (MTBF).
- *Maintainable*—maintainability can be expressed as meantime-to-repair (MTTR).
- *Available*—using the above two concepts availability of a system can be expressed as:

$$\text{System Availability} = \frac{\text{MTBF}}{\text{MTBF} + \text{MTTR}}$$

To design a system which meets these requirements it is necessary first to specify the functional requirements of the system in non-ADP terms. Such a document will address information in the data base, documents to be used, reports to be produced, and production cycles desired.   A design can only begin *after* this document is reasonably complete.

The first step in structured design is to break up the application into functional components which are:

1. Manageably small
2. Solvable separately
3. Easily related to the application

These "chunks" of the problem can be thought of as black boxes in which highly interrelated parts of the problem are in the same "chunk." Unrelated parts of the problem are placed in separate boxes. They are combined in the form of a structured chart. A structured chart is essentially a time independent model of the system. An example of a

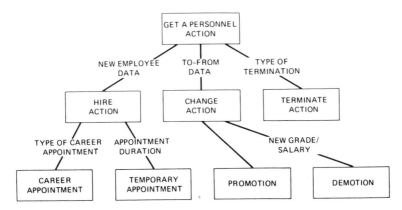

Figure 1. Structure chart for a personnel data entry system.

structure chart is shown in Figure 1. The boxes are the modules, the connecting lines denote the basic flows.

The next step is to analyze the information flow. The previous step isolated the primary processing functions of the system, the high level inputs and high level outputs. The purpose of this phase is to analyze the information flow rather than the procedural flow. Data is expressed on a chart which is referred to as a transform analysis chart. The purpose of the chart is to factor the information flow in terms of *afferent* and *efferent* elements. Afferent elements are those high-level elements which are furthest removed from physical input.   Efferent data elements are those furthest removed from physical outputs—these may be regarded as "logical output data." This usually leaves something in the middle—central transforms—which is the main work of the system. A schematic diagram of the process of transform analysis is shown in Figure 2.

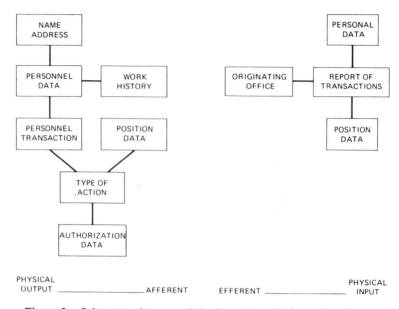

Figure 2. Schematic diagram of the factoring of information flow.

Having addressed the functional requirements of the system and the corresponding data flow, the system designer might pull both of these concepts together in the form of a design. This process has led to a development cycle which corresponds to three phases which can be described as:

- *Structural Design.* Determines what *all* the components are, what each will do, and how the whole lot will be arranged. This phase specifies that some piece of the system will be required at a certain location. It does not specify any technical requirements such as programming language and communication requirements.
- *Communication Analysis.* Refines the completed structural design and selects appropriate communication means such as intermediate files, subroutine argument or external variables.
- *Packaging.* Specifies an efficient and practical way to package each component into a practical program entity (e.g., macro stand-alone program, callable sub-program, etc.).

We have, thus, reduced the system design process to an inter-active three-step process. The format in which these steps are recorded is not so important as the fact that the design process is undertaken in this manner.

The process just described roughly corresponds to the general system design process. We would expect a feasibility study to have been completed and the functional requirements to have been fully examined prior to beginning any of the design activities previously discussed. The product of this design should then provide all the required information and system structure to begin the detail design stage.

When using structured design concepts, the objective of the detail design stage is to translate the use-oriented general design into a data processing-oriented detail design of sufficient completeness, correctness, and clarity to permit the preparation of computer programs. This translation should be performed by continuing the HIPO diagrams produced for the general design. That is, extending them to lower hierarchical levels. The general design may, for example, specify the function "compute gross pay," but the detail design should specify the formulas and conditions under which each formula is to be used to compute gross pay, or any of its component parts. The detail design should also specify record formats, both input and output. At the end of the detail design stage all inputs and outputs should be identified and their formats established and all processes identified and the transactions to be processed and their processing requirements identified.

III. STRUCTURED DESIGN REVIEWS

A. REVIEW METHODOLOGY

Structured design practices differ from customary design practices in three respects:
  1. The stages of the design process are more rigorously defined.
  2. Each stage is followed by a formal design review.
  3. Extensive use is made of functional design aids.
The formal review of a stage shall be conducted using the "structured walk-through" technique. This technique requires that the analysts (programmers) who have performed the stage being reviewed demonstrate the correctness and completeness of their work by walking test transactions through the design logic. Given correct and adequate test data each path through the logic can be demonstrated and proven correct.

The reviewers should include the users of the system for the review of the requirements definition and the general design. The reviewers of the detail design should include the analyst(s) responsible for the general design. The programming logic should be reviewed by the analyst(s) responsible for the detail design of the system. The review of the operations documentation should include the operations personnel who will have to live with the system.

The in-process review is an important development management device. In-process review scheduling is at the discretion of the manager. An in-process review is required at the end of each stage as stated earlier. In addition, they may be specified during project planning to be held at intervals which are compatible with the size of the development being undertaken. For example, a project development stage which is estimated to extend over a period of six months is certainly a candidate for review before its scheduled completion.

The project manager is responsible for preparing and conducting the in-process review. He is responsible for seeing to it that all matters for decision are surfaced and decisions requested. Major points presented, requests for decisions, and agreements made are to be summarized in a written record and distributed to all principals attending.

The manager or an appointed representative will attend the review to insure that the meeting is professionally conducted, and all necessary decisions are made without undue delay. He will make certain that non-technical user-representatives are made as aware as possible of the project progress, and that their views are seriously solicited and considered.

B. REQUIREMENTS DEFINITION REVIEW

The requirements definition-analysis remains the first step in the development process. The review of the requirements definition-analysis should be based on the analyst describing to the user(s) of the system, and the manager, the outputs, inputs, sources of input data, time constraints, and cost constraints associated with the user requirements.

The review process should follow the methodology described in (A) above.

C. GENERAL DESIGN REVIEW

The review of the general design should be based on the analyst(s) walking a group of test-transactions through the logic in order to demonstrate to the user(s) and manager that the design does in fact fulfill the requirements of the problem. The same group of test transactions should also be used in the subsequent reviews.

D. DETAIL DESIGN REVIEW

The review of the detail design should be based on the analyst(s) performing the detail design stage by walking the test transactions through the detail design in order to demonstrate to the analyst(s) who performed the general design that the detail design is correct. In the event that the general design analysts and the detail design analysts are the same, this test shall be demonstrated to the satisfaction of the manager.

E. PROGRAMMING REVEIW

The programming review shall be held on completion of the short HIPO diagrams for the programs and before any actual coding is performed. The senior programmer shall walk through the program logic, using the test transactions.

Actual coding shall follow the top-down concept, in which each level of the Job Control Language (JCL) and code is tested before work proceeds to the next level. Strict adherence to this concept eliminates the need to integrate the system on completion of coding and eliminates the adjustments inevitable when using customary coding practices. As part of the coding process, the programmers shall prepare complete operating instructions for the system. On completion of the coding and testing of the code, an operating instructions review shall be held.

F. OPERATING INSTRUCTIONS REVIEW

The operating instructions review is a two-phase process. *Phase 1* consists of the programmer(s) walking through the complete operating cycle of the system, from start to finish, with equal emphasis given to the activities required on the part of operations personnel under normal conditions and under error condtions. Once the operations personnel reviewing the instructions are satisfied that they seem to be correct and adequate, Phase 1 is complete. *Phase 2* consists of a competent senior operator running the entire system, from start to finish, with no intervention required on the part of the programming staff. Any situations which force the operator to consult with the programmers shall be re-documented in such a manner that the operator can handle the situation without any assistance.

PRACTICE 0220
SYSTEM DEVELOPMENT CYCLE DOCUMENTATION GUIDELINE

CONTENTS

I. INTRODUCTION

    A. GENERAL
    B. PURPOSE

II. SYSTEM REQUIREMENTS STUDY

    A. GENERAL
    B. SPECIFIC

        1. PURPOSE OF DOCUMENT
        2. CURRENT SYSTEM DESCRIPTION
        3. PROBLEMS WITH CURRENT SYSTEM
        4. ALTERNATIVE DESIGN APPROACHES
        5. SYSTEM REQUIREMENTS AND
            CAPABILITIES
        6. MANAGEMENT ISSUES
        7. SYSTEM CONSTRAINTS
        8. CONCEPTUAL DESIGN OF PROPOSED
            SYSTEM
        9. IMPLEMENTATION PLAN

III. SYSTEM DESIGN NOTEBOOK

    A. GENERAL
    B. SPECIFIC

        1. SYSTEM FLOW
        2. HIPO

3. DATA BASE   7
4. INPUT/OUTPUT   9
5. CONTROL LOGIC   10
6. TEST PLAN   10
7. JCL   10
8. PROGRAM SUMMARIES   10

FIGURE 1: SYSTEM REQUIREMENTS STUDY
           TABLE OF CONTENTS   2
FIGURE 2: CONTENT OF SYSTEM DESIGN
           NOTEBOOK   5
FIGURE 3: INPUT CROSS-REFERENCE MATRIX   6
FIGURE 4: FILE CROSS-REFERENCE MATRIX   6
FIGURE 5: OUTPUT CROSS-REFERENCE MATRIX   6
FIGURE 6: DATA ELEMENT VALIDATION
           CHART   8
FIGURE 7: PROGRAM SUMMARY SHEET   10

I. INTRODUCTION

A. GENERAL

This guideline defines a comprehensive set of documentation to be developed throughout the system development cycle. It can be followed for developments, using both conventional and structured development approaches.

Because of resource limitations and differences in project scope, it may be only practical to develop a subset of the total documentation called for in this practice. Therefore, agreement shall be made on a project-by-project basis as to the exact documentation to be developed for the specific project.

The components of the system documentation are:
1. System Requirements Study
2. System Design Notebook
3. Production Control Run Book

The first two components are outlined in this practice. The third is described in a separate practice (see Production Control Run Book practice).

B. PURPOSE

This practice is a comprehensive outline of the documentation required for a new system development project or a major overhaul of an existing system. It specifies the documentation which is required to augment the Short HIPO documentation.

II. SYSTEM REQUIREMENTS STUDY

A. GENERAL

The System Requirements Study is the principal formal documentation derived from the investigative study stage. It will be a stand-alone document.

TABLE OF CONTENTS

1. *Purpose of Document*

2. *Current System Description*

3. *Problems with Current System*

4. *Alternative Design Approaches*

5. *System Requirements and Capabilities*

6. *Management Issues*

7. *System Constraints*

8. *Conceptual Design of Proposed System*

9. *Implementation Plan*

Figure 1. System requirements study table of contents.

B. SPECIFIC

A sample Table of Contents for the System Requirements Study is shown in Figure 1 and discussed below:

1. *Purpose of Document*

Describe *why* the current system needs revision or upgrade. State specific intention of this document (e.g., critical issues remaining to be addressed).

2. *Current System Description*

Describe the current situation, i.e., the capabilities of the current system. For example:
   a. Types of output
   b. Data entry

    c. Selective reporting
    d. Audit trail
    e. Summary data
    f. Trend reporting
    g. Available reports

3. *Problems with Current System*

Describe specific weaknesses of current system. For example:
    a. Responsive to user needs
    b. Data validity
    c. Timeliness of data
    d. Usefulness of outputs
    e. Operational costs

4. *Alternative Design Approaches*

Describe briefly various possible approaches to solving the problems
described in (3) above.

5. *System Requirements and Capabilities*

Describe the specific requirement of the new or revised system.
This description shall include:
    a. Getting data into the system
    b. Information reporting and use
    c. Technical improvements

6. *Management Issues*

Describe critical issues that will affect the operational effectiveness
of the system. Indicate specific management actions required.

7. *System Constraints*

Describe specific factors that will impact on the implementation of
the system. For example:
    a. Interfaces with other systems
    b. Hardware procurement
    c. Availability of data
    d. Software development
    e. Software procurement

8. *Conceptual Design of Proposed System*

Describe the critical aspects of the system design and present an
overview of the system in diagramatic form. The description shall
contain the following subsections:
    a. *General System Description.* Describe major processing steps.
    b. *System Input.* Describe forms or CRT masks on which data is
       to be captured.
    c. *Computer Processing.* Describe, in simple terms, main compo-
       nents of computer processing.

9. *Implementation Plan*

Describe major phases of development and provide milestone schedule of major events.

III. SYSTEM DESIGN NOTEBOOK (SDN)

A. GENERAL

This document is created during the ongoing development work of the General Design, Detail Design, Development, and Implementation stages of a project. It shall be divided into a three-ring binder having, as a minimum, the following dividers:[1]

1. System Flow   5. Control Logic
2. HIPO   6. Test Plan
3. Data Base   7. JCL
4. Input/Output   8. Program summaries[2]

The outline of the content of this notebook is contained in Figure 2.

[1]Oversize program documentation (e.g., source program listings) shall be maintained in a separate binder for all system programs.
[2]For large systems, the program summaries may be kept in a separate binder.

System Design Notebook Divider	Stage	Topic	Documentation
System Flow	General design	a. System flowchart	Flow diagram
	General design	b. System interface charts	Relationship of data elements, programs, files, etc.
HIPO	General design	a. Functional hierarchy	Top level HIPO Virtual Table of Contents
	General design	b. Functional overview diagrams	Processing steps in top level functions
	Detail design	c. Detail functional diagrams	Expansion of Virtual Table of Contents (VTOC) and associated functional diagrams
Data Base	General design	a. Data element description	Data field listing
	General design	b. Data element validation	Validation chart
		c. Data base overview	

Figure 2. Content of system design notebook.

System Design Notebook Divider	Stage	Topic	Documentation
	Detail design	d. Data base organization	Data base structure
	Detail design	e. Data element specifications	Data element format specifications
	Detail design	f. File characteristics	File specification
Input/Output	General design	a. Input/output description	Identification of the content of system inputs and reports
	Detail design	b. Layouts	Document or CRT layout
Control Logic	Detail design	a. Control logic	Program control structure
Test Plan	Development	a. Test plan	Testing strategy and specific tests
JCL	Development	a. Test JCL	Listing
	Implementation	b. Production JCL	Annotated listing
Program Summaries	Implementation	a. Program summary	Program summary sheet

Figure 2. (*continued*)

B. SPECIFIC

The documentation that falls within each notebook divider is described in the subsequent subsections as it would be developed during the stages of the system development cycle.

1. *System Flow (Divider)*

a. *System Flowchart* (General Design)
Show in flowchart form, supplemented by narrative as needed, the overall flow of information from various sources, transformation of data into machine-readable subsystem processing, updating of data base, output reports, and distribution of output to final destination.

b. *System Interface Charts* (General Design)
Develop a series of matrix charts to show the action, usage, and appearance of data elements. These charts facilitate tracing the logic of the system in program development and maintenance. It is suggested that the following types of charts be developed as needed depending on the complexity of the system:
  • Data Element to INPUT

- Data Element to FILE
- Data Element to OUTPUT

Examples of the three charts are shown in Figures 3, 4, and 5 respectively.

2. *HIPO* (Divider)

   a. *Functional Hierarchy: Virtual Table of Contents* (VTOC) (General Design)

Show in chart form the hierarchy of the system functions to be performed. This chart shall be limited to major user processing functions and, therefore, should roughly break down the system functions into the major sub-processes within program modules. The VTOC shall be prepared according to the guidelines presented in the Short HIPO Documentation Guideline practice.

   b. *Functional Overview Diagrams* (General Design)

Prepare the functional diagrams as specified in the Short HIPO Documentation Guideline practice for functions identified in the VTOC. (See Figures 2 and 3, Practice 0310, pp. 109-110.

System Name:_____

Data Element .Input .Doc.	Source Document 1	Source Document 2	Source Document 3	Source Document 4	Etc.
Field A					
Field B					
Field C					
Field D					
Etc.					

Legend:

U=Unmodified move
M=Modified move
C=Conditional move (user optional)

Figure 3. Input cross-reference matrix.

Explain the condition logic under which the processing steps will be executed as well as important exceptions to normal processing in an extended description.

c. *Detail Functional Diagrams* (Detail Design)

If the system is complex, or is to be programmed under contract, the functional documentation should be expanded to a more detailed level (one or two levels) as described in the Short HIPO Documentation Guideline.

3. *Data Base* (Divider)

a. *Data Element Description* (General Design)

Identify the data elements which will be contained in the system data base. Give their full name and brief description. If the element serves as a linkage between files, or as an accessory, then explain. Develop a data dictionary for the data base (use the Date Dictionary practice.)

b. *Data Element Validation* (General Design)

Describe the criteria for editing the data elements, specifying the conditions under which the data elements will be valid. See Figure 6 for a sample chart.

System Name:_____

.Data .File Data Element	File 1	File 2	File 3	File 4	Etc.
Field A					
Field B					
Field C					
Field D					
Etc.					

Legend:

```
G=Generated
M=Modified
R=Reference
C=Calculated
```

Figure 4. File cross-reference matrix.

System Name:_____

Data Element .Output .Re- .port .	Report 1	Report 2	Report 3	Report 4	Etc.
Field A					
Field B					
Field C					
Field D					
Etc.					

Legend:

U=Unmodified move
M=Modified move
C=Conditional move (User optional)

Figure 5. Output cross-reference matrix.

System Name:_____

Input Source	Data Element Name	Blank (Not) Required)	Numeric	Alpha	Alpha-Numeric	In Code Table	Not In Code Table	Comments
	Program code	X	X			X		
	Est. com-pletion date	X	X					

Figure 6. Data element validation chart.

c. *Data Base Overview* (General Design)

Illustrate the relationship of the data base files to the applications that call upon these files. A particular effective way of showing this is to have a diagram that both shows the relationship of the files to one another, and the set of files used in each application. A good method is to draw a borderline around the files belonging to one application. Files common to more than one application can be immediately seen. The application borders can be color coded to aid rapid assimilation of the relationships.

d. *Data Base Organization* (Detail Design)

(1) *Logical Structures*

Show a graphical representation of the logical organization. (This is an optional requirement and would depend on the complexity of the data base. See the Data Base Administrator practice for further amplification.)

(2) *File Groupings*

In addition to a schematic, list the date elements which will appear within each data base file.

e. *Data Element Specifications* (Detail Design)

Provide a detail specification of the data element. For example, under the INQUIRE information retrieval system, the Data Definition Table Form is utilized to describe the parameters of the data element. The items specified include the field size, format, and number of occurences.

f. *File Characteristics* (Detail Design)

Specify the characteristics of the system files. This specification should include:

- Brief (one or two line) description of file purpose.
- Access keys
- Period size
- Blocking factor
- Retention cycle
- Disk file system residency (temporary or permanent)
- Backup requirements (frequency)
- Security classification

4. *Input/Output* (Divider)

a. *Input/Output Description* (General Design)

For each input:

- List data elements

Four each output:

- List data elements
- Describe report organization
- Identify report breakpoints (e.g., subtotals).

b. *Layouts* (Detail Design)

Provide layout (card, printer spacing, form, or CRT mask) for all *standard* system input and output. Show either actual data or dummy data that will illustrate how output displays will look.

5. *Control Logic* (Divider) (Detail Design)

Draw a diagram or provide an ALGOL-like narrative, which defines a sequence and/or conditions under which the functional subprocesses of the program module will be performed. (NOTE: This control structure logic may be contained in the HIPO Extended Descriptions.)

6. *Test Plan* (Divider) (Development)

For major system development projects a test plan shall be developed which includes as a minimum the overall testing

```
1.  PROGRAM NUMBER_ _ _ _ _ _ _ _ _ _   2.  Program ID:_ _ _ _ _ _ _
                                             (in JCL)

3.  PROGRAM NAME_ _ _ _ _ _ _ _ _ _ _ _ _ _ _ _ _ _ _ _ _ _ _ _ _ _

4.  INPUT/OUTPUT FILES:
    __       DSN (in JCL)   In  Out |   __    DSN (in JCL)        In  Out
   |__| _ _ _ _ _ _ _ _ _   _   _   |  |__| _ _ _ _ _ _ _ _ _ _   _   _

   |__| _ _ _ _ _ _ _ _ _   _   _   |  |__| _ _ _ _ _ _ _ _ _ _   _   _

   |__| _ _ _ _ _ _ _ _ _   _   _   |  |__| _ _ _ _ _ _ _ _ _ _   _   _

   |__| _ _ _ _ _ _ _ _ _   _   _   |  |__| _ _ _ _ _ _ _ _ _ _   _   _

   |__| _ _ _ _ _ _ _ _ _   _   _   |  |__| _ _ _ _ _ _ _ _ _ _   _   _

   |__| _ _ _ _ _ _ _ _ _   _   _   |  |__| _ _ _ _ _ _ _ _ _ _   _   _

   |__| _ _ _ _ _ _ _ _ _   _   _   |  |__| _ _ _ _ _ _ _ _ _ _   _   _

   |__| _ _ _ _ _ _ _ _ _   _   _   |  |__| _ _ _ _ _ _ _ _ _ _   _   _


5.  PROGRAM SUMMARY:







8.  SPECIAL LOGIC/INTERFACE:






9.  REPORTS PRODUCED:    |__| None   |__| See attached
```

Figure 7. Program summary sheet.

strategy, a brief description of specific tests to be performed, and a listing of the test data base.

7. *JCL* (Divider)

   a. *Test JCL* (Development)
   A copy of the *test* JCL.
   b. *Production JCL* (Implementation)
   A copy of the *production* JCL.

8. *Program Summaries* (Divider) (Implementation)

For each program in the system, complete a summary sheet describing the principal component logic. (See Figure 7.) Refer also to Figure 1, Naming Conventions, in the Job Control Language Standards practice.

The instructions for completing this sheet are:

   a. *Program Number*
   Sequential number assigned program in the runstream (if any used).

   b. *Program ID*
   Abbreviated name used in JCL PROC (see Figure 1 in the Job Control Language Standards practice).

   c. *Program Name*
   Full descriptive name.

   d. *Input/Output Files*
   Provide abbreviated name as used in JCL PROC (see Figure 1 in the Job Control Language Standards practice) and indicate whether this program READS FROM (in) or WRITES TO (out) or both.

   e. *Program Summary*
   A brief encapsulation of the program purpose within the sequence, including the conditions under which it is executed, and principal functions.

   f. *Special Logic/Interfaces*
   Describe exception logic, if any, or complex coding found in the program. Indicate interfaces with other programs in the system.

   g. *Reports Produced*
   Indicate whether this program produces any reports and attach a copy.

PRACTICE 0230
STRUCTURED COBOL GUIDELINE

CONTENTS

I. INTRODUCTION

    A. GENERAL
    B. PURPOSE

II. GENERAL INSTRUCTIONS

    A. SOURCE STATEMENT NUMBERING

III. IDENTIFICATION DIVISION

    A. PROGRAM ID
    B. AUTHOR
    C. INSTALLATION
    D. DATE WRITTEN
    E. DATE COMPILED
    F. PROGRAM SYNOPSIS
    G. PROGRAM SWITCHES
    H. PROGRAM OPTIONS
    I. PROGRAM LIMITATIONS
    J. UNUSUAL CODING
    K. PROGRAM MODIFICATION LOG

IV. ENVIRONMENT DIVISION

    A. SELECT
    B. FILE NAMES, ASSIGN, AND DEVICE NAMES
    C. FILES NAMES

V. DATA DIVISION

A. CATALOGED ENTRIES
B. FD ENTRIES
C. RECORD DESCRIPTION ENTRIES
D. WORKING STORAGE

VI. PROCEDURE DIVISION

A. GENERAL ORGANIZATION
B. HIERARCHY
C. CONTROL SECTION
D. COMMON PROCEDURES SECTION
E. SELF-CONTAINED SECTIONS
F. INDEPENDENT SEGMENTS
G. FORMAT
H. ALLOWABLE PROGRAM STRUCTURES
I. STRUCTURED PROGRAMMING PROHIBITION

FIGURE 1: COBOL CODING FORM
FIGURE 2: COBOL CODING FORM

I. INTRODUCTION

A. GENERAL

This practice prescribes a standard format, content, and organization of COBOL source programs. It is designed especially for structured programming technique, but is also highly recommended for use in all COBOL programs.

B. PURPOSE

This practice establishes a standardized method of writing COBOL programs. It is a guide to all COBOL program development for internally developed and contractually developed programs. While it is not mandatory to follow the guidelines, it is designed to facilitate program maintenance by having all programs have a common structure.

II. GENERAL INSTRUCTIONS

A. SOURCE STATEMENT NUMBERING

All source statements shall be numbered in ascending sequence with a gap of 100 between consecutive numbers.

III. IDENTIFICATION DIVISION

A. PROGRAM ID

The program name assigned by the data base administrator (or project manager) shall be used.

B. AUTHOR

The name and organizational unit of the programmer shall be entered.

C. INSTALLATION

The name of the user organization shall be entered.

D. DATE WRITTEN

The month, day, and year of completion of the program shall be entered.

E. DATE COMPILED

The date shall be entered.

F. PROGRAM SYNOPSIS

A narrative describing the functions performed by the program shall be included as remarks and required in *all* programs.

G. PROGRAM SWITCHES

A brief explanation of the use of program switches is to be included as a comment.

H. PROGRAM OPTIONS

An explanation of the options, the circumstances under which they are to be used, and how they are invoked is to be included as a comment.

I. PROGRAM LIMITATIONS

Limitations on input volumes, table sizes, etc. are to be specified as a comment.

J. UNUSUAL CODING

"Tricky routines" are to be renamed, and either described, or the documentation describing the technique used shall be referenced in this comment.

K. PROGRAM MODIFICATION LOG

A brief entry specifying the date of each change (month and year), the author's initials, and the reason for the change shall be made for each change made in the program. This should be strictly adhered to, particularly for programs adopting full structured programming methodology.

IV. ENVIRONMENT DIVISION

A. SELECT

Each SELECT statement shall begin in position 12; therefore, each SELECT statement shall begin on a new line.

B. FILE NAMES, ASSIGN, AND DEVICE NAMES

These entries in the SELECT statements shall be aligned vertically.

C. FILE NAMES

File names shall be assigned by the data base administrator (or project manager).

V. DATA DIVISION

A. CATALOGED ENTRIES

1. In the event that an FD or 01 level WORKING STORAGE entry is used in more than one program, it shall be cataloged by the data base administrator (or project manager).
2. The replacing option of the copy shall not be used when the library entries are included in the DATA DIVISION.
3. The library name shall be specified by the data base administrator (or project manager) when library entries are included in the DATA DIVISION.

B. FD ENTRIES

1. Each clause shall be on a separate line.
2. The order of the clauses shall be:
   a. BLOCK CONTAINS
   b. RECORD CONTAINS
   c. LABEL RECORD(S)
   d. DATA RECORD(S)
   e. REPORT
   f. LINAGE

```
 _____
|    SEQUENCE    |                                                          |
| (Page)|(Serial)|                                                          |
|       |        |01   PERSONNEL-REC.                                       |
|       |        |                                                          |
|       |        |     05   IDENTIFIERS.                                    |
|       |        |          10 EMP-NUM           PIC 9(6).                  |
|       |        |          10 SOC-SEC-NUM       PIC 9(9).                  |
|       |        |          10 EMP-NAME                                     |
|       |        |             15  LAST-NAME     PIC A(20).                 |
|       |        |             15  FIRST-NAME    PIC A(11).                 |
|       |        |             15  MIDDLE-INIT   PIC A.                     |
|       |        |             15  NAME-SUFFIX   PIC X(4).                  |
|       |        |     05   CLASSIFICATION-DATA                             |
|       |        |          10  DEPT-NO          PIC 9(3).                  |
|       |        |          10  JOB-CODE         PIC 9(3).                  |
|       |        |     05   MAILING-ADDRESS.                                |
|       |        |          10  CITY             PIC A(15).                 |
|       |        |          10  STATE            PIC AA.                    |
|       |        |          10  ZIP              PIC 9(5).                  |
|       |  165   |          10  STREET           PIC X(20).                 |
|_____|_____|_____|
```

Figure 1. Cobol coding form.

C. RECORD DESCRIPTION ENTRIES

1. Level numbers shall be consecutive: i.e., 01, 02, etc.
2. Level numbers shall be indented four positions (1 tab stop for terminal devices) for each subordinate level.
3. Record entries shall be indented and aligned in a manner which will facilitate reading the program.
4. PICTURE clauses are to aligned vertically, if at all possible. (See Figure 1.)

D. WORKING STORAGE

1. Level 77 entries shall not be used.
    NOTE: This applies only to structured programming.
2. Numeric values used in computations, as indexes, etc., shall be contained on one level 01 record.
3. Each report header and/or trailer line shall be contained in an 01 record and shall be a complete representation of the output line.
4. WORKING STORAGE entries normally shall be initialized with a VALUE clause unless a REDEFINE clause is used.

VI. PROCEDURE DIVISION

This guide to program organization is intended to facilitate user understanding for those who are not authors of the programs. Particularly for programs adopting full structured programming methodology, this guide should be rigorously followed.

A. **GENERAL ORGANIZATION**

1. The PROCEDURE DIVISION shall be ordered as follows:
   a. Declaratives Section
   b. Control Section
   c. Common Procedures Section
   d. Self-Contained Sections
   e. Independent Segments
2. All code used for initialization shall be contained in an Independent Segment.
3. All code used for end-of-job processing shall be contained in an Independent Segment.

B. **HIERARCHY**

1. The PROCEDURE DIVISION shall be hierarchical in nature, with each hierarchical level corresponding to a hierarchical level on the design tree of HIPO diagram for the program.
2. Each Self-Contained Section shall correspond to a hierarchical level, except for the top level, and, except at the bottom level, shall contain its own Control Section, analagous to the Program Control Section and subordinate level Self-Contained Sections. Bottom level Self-Contained Sections shall not have Control Sections.
3. A Self-Contained Section may also contain a Common Section, whose modules are local to itself and not used outside of the Self-Contained Section.
4. Independent Segments, although physically separate, if logically associated with only one Self-Contained Section, are considered part of the Self-Contained Section.

C. **CONTROL SECTION**

1. The Self-Contained Sections associated with a specific Control Section may be executed only from the Control Section.
2. A Control Section may not directly execute Self-Contained Sections immediately subordinate to any other Control Section.
3. A Control Section, on completion, may either reiterate or return to the next higher level Control Section which invoked it.

D. **COMMON PROCEDURES SECTION**

1. Common Procedures are those performed from more than one place in the program.
2. The Common Procedures Section shall be reserved for procedures not local to any one Self-Contained Section.

3. A Common Procedure may be performed from any place in the program at any time.

4. A Common Procedure may perform another Common Procedure.

5. A Common Procedure may not execute either a Control Section or a Self-Contained Section of code.

6. With the exception of encountering a fatal error, all Common Procedures must return to their caller on completion, hence Common Procedures may not be branched to but must be performed.

E. SELF-CONTAINED SECTIONS

1. Self-Contained Sections may consist of Control Sections and one or more lower level Self-Contained Sections.

2. A Self-Contained Section may be executed only from the immediately higher level Control Section and on completion must return to that Control Section, hence Self-Contained Sections may not be branched to but must be performed.

3. A Self-Contained Section may perform a Common Procedure or Independent Segment.

4. A Self-Contained Section may neither perform nor branch to another Self-Contained Section at the same or higher hierarchical level, except that immediately subordinate Self-Contained Sections may be performed by the Control Section of a Self-Contained Section.

5. The use of GO TO is permitted providing that the branch target is contained within the same Self-Contained Section at the same level.

F. INDEPENDENT SEGMENTS

1. Independent Segments consist of seldom used procedures which are either logically independent or which are logically dependent and physically independent from any Self-Contained Segment.

2. The specification of a segment number in the range 50 to 99 will cause the code section which follows to be treated as an overlayable Independent Segment by COBOL.

3. Independent Segments shall be treated as though they are Common Procedures, since the only difference is that an Independent Segment may be in an overlay while the Common Procedure is always memory resident.

G. FORMAT

1. Each section and paragraph name shall be preceded by a comment statement which briefly describes the function performed

in the section or paragraph.   The statement is to be preceded and followed by a blank line.

2. Indentation rules are:

   a. Section and paragraph names shall begin in Column 8.

   b. Declaratives, Common Procedures, Independent Segments, and top level Control Section executable statements shall begin in Column 12.

   c. The Self-Contained Section executable statements shall be indented four columns in from their Control Section statements and the statements in each Control Section shall be idented four columns from the statements in the immediately superior Control Section.

3. Names used in the program for sections and paragraphs should coincide, if possible, with those used in the design tree or the HIPO diagram.   Names should also indicate the function performed in the section or paragraph.   Thus a section found at block ABE on a design tree which computes state and local tax should be named:

   ABE-COMP-TAX

4. Each statement shall begin on a new line.

5. Continuations of statements shall be indented two spaces so that they may be readily distinguished from adjacent statements at the same and lower hierarchical levels.

6. Conditional statements shall be formatted as follows:

   a. First line—Condition

   b. Second line—Indented three spaces; the true action(s).

   c. Third line—(Vertically aligned with the condition IF.)   The key word ELSE followed by the false action(s).

H.   ALLOWABLE PROGRAM STRUCTURES

The PROCEDURE DIVISION of each program shall consist exclusively of code segments organized into the five structures generally accepted under the tenets of structured programming:

1. A SEQUENCE structure is a logically self-contained segment of code with only one entry point and only one exit point.   A SEQUENCE may perform procedures not physically contained

```
    IF YTD-FICA < FICA-LIMIT
       THEN PERFORM COMPUTE -FICA
       IF YTD-FICA > FICA-LIMIT
          THEN COMPUTE WK-FICA = WK-FICA + FICA-LIMIT - YTD-FICA
          MOVE FICA-LIMIT TO YTD-FICA
       ELSE GO TO NO-FICA
    ELSE GO TO NO-FICA.

 NO-FICA.
```

Figure 2.   Cobol coding form.

within itself, and may contain sequences of statements other than branching and conditional statements.

2. An IFTHENELSE structure consists of one or more levels of IF statement. The code executed under the various conditions shall consist of other valid structures and performed procedures with the proviso that all such code return to the end of the IFTHENELSE structure. (See Figure 2.)

3. A DOWHILE structure is, technically, one in which a condition is tested and if true a sequence of steps performed. The process is reiterated until the condition is no longer satisfied. In COBOL the DOWHILE shall be implemented by using the PERFORM... UNTIL... verb with the condition negated. For example, to DOWHILE A is true;

    PERFORM < procedure-name > UNTIL NOT A.

4. A DOUNTIL structure is, technically, one in which a process is performed and after the processing a condition is tested. If the condition is not met the process and test are reiterated. In COBOL the DOUNTIL shall be implemented by using the PERFORM... UNTIL... verb. Note that COBOL tests the condition before performing the procedure. Therefore an unconditional PERFORM is required to assume that the procedure is executed at least one time. For example, to DOUNTIL A is true;

    PERFORM < procedure-name >.
    PERFORM < procedure-name > UNTIL A.

5. The CASE structure provides for a multiple target branch, with the branch target being determined by the value contained in a variable at the time the CASE is entered. In COBOL the CASE structure is implemented with the DEPENDING option of the GO (GO TO) verb. For example, if the variable being tested is grade level in school, and targets are Elementary School (ELEM). Intermediate School (INT). and High School (HS), the CASE structure would be:

    GO ELEM,ELEM,ELEM,ELEM,ELEM,ELEM,INT,INT,HS,
        HS,HS,HS
    DEPENDING ON GRADE-LEVEL.

I. **STRUCTURED PROGRAMMING PROHIBITION**

1. The following COBOL verbs shall not be used under any conditions:

    ALTER
    ENTER

2. Every effort must be made to avoid the use of GO (GO TO) except in the CASE structure. Note that if the use of the GO (GO TO) will increase the clarity of the program, it is preferable to use the GO (GO TO) rather than develop an artificial and confushing sequence of code, in order to avoid the use of GO (GO TO).

PRACTICE 0240
EDIT AND VALIDATION SPECIFICATION

CONTENTS

I. INTRODUCTION

    A. GENERAL
    B. PURPOSE

II. EDIT AND VALIDATION PROCEDURES

III. EDITING RULES

    A. SELF-CHECKING CODES
    B. CONTENT AND FORMAT TEST
    C. LIMIT TESTS
    D. ACTUAL VALUE TESTS
    E. COMPOSITION CHECK
    F. LOGICAL RELATIONSHIP TEST
    G. PRESENCE TESTING
    H. MATCHING TESTS
    I. SET COMPLETION TESTS
    J. RELATED TRANSACTION TESTS
    K. COMPLETENESS CHECK (BATCH)
    L. SEQUENTIAL NUMBERING CHECKS
    M. PAGINATION

IV. VISUAL VERIFICATION

V. ERROR ANALYSIS

FIGURE 1: EDIT CHECKLIST MATRIX
FIGURE 2: SELF-CHECK DIGIT CALCULATION

I. INTRODUCTION

A. GENERAL

This practice describes an edit and validation specification, which shall be prepared for all applications which cause the data base files to be modified. A separate document is needed because there should be only one reference to all error checking procedures to be used on the data. Also, in a transaction programming environment, the editing rules may be contained in a program separate from the program which does the actual updating of the data files.

B. PURPOSE

The purpose of this specification is to define the edit and validation scheme including processing, logic, and specification editing checks, which will be performed on input messages of online systems.

II. EDIT AND VALIDATION PROCEDURES

This section of the specification shall describe the strategy to be followed for error detection and correction.

The accustomed procedure in a batch system is the rejection of the transaction in its entirety, when errors are found in one or more fields. This approach should not be carried over to an online system, where individual fields may be processed and corrected in one operation.

The basic procedure alternatives must be documented. They are:

- Acceptance of the transaction only when all fields pass the edit checks.
- Conditional acceptance of a transaction and insertion into the data base, as long as errors are confined to fields not used as access keys.
- Conditional acceptance of the transaction and storage in a pending file.
- Conditional acceptance of the transaction only when non-critical fields have errors.

The recommended guideline is to devise some kind of conditional acceptance procedure which will avoid rejection of transactions containing errors. One approach is to provide the operator with a special SAVE command that would cause the record to be placed in a conditional status, in a special hold file, or in the data base proper.

In specifying a particular procedure, the efficiency of the error detection and correction scheme should be maximized, without compromising the integrity of the data base.

Application_____

TESTS	X	X	X	X	X	X	X	X
1. Self-checking Code								
2. Content and Format Test								
3. Limit								
4. Actual Value								
5. Composition								
6. Logical Relationship								
7. Presence								
8. Matching								
9. Set Completion								
10. Related Transaction								
11. Batch Completeness								
12. Sequential Numbering Checks								
13. Pagination								

PREPARED BY_____   DATE_____   APPROVED BY_____   DATE_____

Figure 1. Edit checklist matrix.

III. EDITING RULES

The editing rules shall be specified in this section. A cover sheet showing which rules will be applied to which data fields is shown in Figure 1. The individual tests named on the form are described below:

A. SELF-CHECKING CODES

A self-checking code number is a code in which the unit's position can be derived from computations using the remaining digits of the code number as operands.

The self-checking scheme, which currently is most commonly used in the data processing industry, is a simple scheme which will catch transposition of digits by performing a calculation on odd position digits in the number.

Figure 2 illustrates the procedure used to generate the check digit using this scheme. Starting at the right-most digit of the code, the odd number digits are each doubled. If the result of any of the doubling operations is greater than 9, the two digits (in the result) are added;

Note: IBM keypunches and keyverifiers, with an optional feature, automatically compares the position to the digit keyed in by the operator and locks the keyboard if an error is found.

e.g., 6 + 6 = 12, 1 + 2 = 3. These results are added to the sum of the even number digits. The units position in the summing operation is subtracted from 1 and the result becomes the check digit.

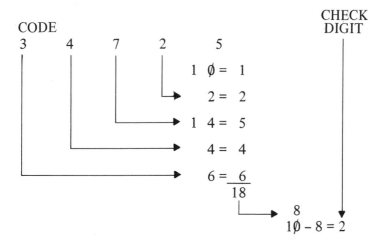

RESULTING SELF CHECKING CODE = 347252

UNIDENTIFIED TRANSPOSITION ERRORS

CODE	CHECK DIGIT	SELF CHECKING CODE
3 4 7 2 5	2	3 4 7 2 5 2
3 4 5 2 7	2	3 4 5 2 7 2
3 2 5 4 7	2	3 2 5 4 7 2
3 2 7 4 5	2	3 2 7 4 5 2
5 4 3 2 7	2	5 4 3 2 7 2
5 4 7 2 3	2	5 4 7 2 3 2
5 2 3 4 7	2	5 2 3 4 7 2
5 2 7 4 3	2	5 2 7 4 3 2
7 2 3 4 5	2	7 2 3 4 5 2
7 2 5 4 3	2	7 2 5 4 3 2
7 4 3 2 5	2	7 4 3 2 5 2
7 4 5 2 3	2	7 4 5 2 3 2

Figure 2. Self-checking digit calculation.

The second section of Figure 2 illustrates all 12 of the transposition errors which would not be detected by the check system scheme. The remaining 108 possible variations of these 5 digits would be detected by the check digit test. Assuming a 5% error rate, the probability of an undetected error in a self-checking code is:

$$.05 \times .10 \text{ or } .005 \text{ or } 1/2 \text{ of } 1\%.$$

This calculation is based on the fact that 10% of all possible combinations of the same set of digits will yield the same check digit, resulting in a 10% probability of a check digit error not being detected. Therefore, there will be an error rate of 5%. While it is theoretically possible to develop a self-checking scheme that will detect 100% of the errors, the degree of complexity required to improve performance of the check digit scheme is not warranted.

A word of caution is appropriate with regard to the error message generated when the code is rejected. One installation displayed the message "Self-check Digit Error." The terminal operators recognized, or looked up, the correct check digit and resubmitted the transaction. In many cases, it was not the check digit but the code that was in error. Transactions were processed against the wrong master records, and the errors perpetuated throughout the system. The error message should have stated "Error in Code Number."

B.   CONTENT AND FORMAT TEST

Two tests that eliminate many errors are the content test and the format test. The content test checks to assure that input fields have been entered as blank. Since it has been determined that a field has contents, the format test is used to determine if the individual character positions are of the expected format; i.e., alphabetic, numeric, or special symbol.

C.   LIMIT TESTS

Unlikely and impossible values can be determined for each amount and/or quantity field by either emperical or statistical techniques. Range limits shall be developed, and the field compared to the limits on input. If the value of the field exceeds the limits of possibility, e.g., over 168 hours worked, it should automatically be rejected. If the field exceeds the limits of probability, but is possible, e.g., hours worked per week in excess of 70 but less than 168, the field should be questioned by the system and the user given an opportunity to make a correction. If the user reenters the same value on the retry, the system should accept it, but should place a message on the system log.

D.   ACTUAL VALUE TESTS

Some data fields have a limited number of possible entries; e.g., sex can be either male or female and, as a result, it is sometimes practical to compare the actual contents of a field against each of the permitted values and reject any field which does not contain a permitted value.

E.   COMPOSITION CHECK

The composition check tests whether all of the data fields expected on a transaction are present. The composition check, generally, should be performed immediately after the end-of-message (EOM) is encountered.

When dealing with free format input, it is possible that the user is "out of phase" for several fields on a record. Thus, the error message generated by the composition check should display each field and the identity which the system has assumed for each field. The error correction routine should require the user to accept, or modify, each of the fields entered, so that the "out of phase" error can be corrected.

F.   LOGICAL RELATIONSHIP TEST

A logical relationship test is one which operates on two or more data fields in one transaction and uses their interrelationship to validate a field. For example, if a transaction includes quantity, rate, and amount, the quantity can be multiplied by the rate and the computed amount used to validate the entered amount. If the amounts match, this indicates that all three fields are correct. If there is a mismatch, it is known that at least one of the three fields is in error.

In other cases, the logical relationship may be indicated by the compatibility of various data fields. For example, an employee whose position code identifies him as exempt, i.e., salaried, cannot have a time-worked number of other than one, or any entry for overtime hours.

G.   PRESENCE TESTING

Even after all of the above tests have been passed, the transaction is not yet ready to be processed. Once the transaction fields and the transactions have been validated as acceptable, it is necessary to verify that the transaction is being made against a valid and active record to avoid compromising the data base. For example, it is possible to delete a master record and then have someone try to process against it later the same day, or worse, it is possible to replace a master record with a different record and process a transaction intended for the initial holder of the code against the later master.

H.   MATCHING TESTS

In addition to determining that a master record is present, it is also necessary to match the contents of the transaction against the contents of the master to verify that the correct record is available for processing. Matching tests are limited to code numbers and descriptive data fields, e.g., sizes, etc.

I.   SET COMPLETION TESTS

The input to some applications consists of a set of transactions as opposed to each transaction being independent. In an order entry system, (e.g., one item), the complete order is entered, one transaction at a time. Under these circumstances, the system should also validate that the entire set is complete and accurate. This can be accomplished by having the user enter a "set total" message at the end of each set.

1. Count Test

In the count test, the first test performed, the count on the "set total" transaction is compared to the transaction count maintained by the system. If the counts agree, then any other discrepancies reflect data errors rather than omissions. If the counts disagree, the user should be notified and given the opportunity to verify and correct the count.

If, after correction, the counts still do not agree, then the number of transactions entered is incorrect and further discrepancies are the result of having either too few or too many transactions. The error messages cue the user in detecting errors. The following messages might be used for this purpose.

Transactions Count over by   1 - Transactions entered twice?
Transactions Count over by   20 - Page entered twice?
Transactions Count under by   1 - Transaction omitted?
Transactions Count under by 20 - Page not entered?

2. Total Test

Most applications documents contain totals which may be compared to totals for the same items which are accumulated during processing. Typically, dollar amounts are totaled, and other fields, such as quantity and weight, can be totaled.

Because most common errors in completeness are the result of entering a single transaction twice or the omission of a single transaction, a display of the discrepancy amount will often allow for quick error isolation.

3. Hash Totals

Hash totals are totals of data fields which are only for error detection and correction. For example, the accumulation of code numbers is of no value in the processing of a set of transactions except to identify the code number of a transaction which has either been entered twice or omitted.

Although hash total discrepancies enable the most rapid and accurate means of pinpointing the specific incorrect transaction, their accumulation may place an additional and unacceptable burden on the user. Hash totals should not be used unless input accuracy becomes a problem.

J. RELATED TRANSACTION TESTS

The presence of a transaction of one type often indicates that a transaction of a different type should also be present in the set. For istance, in a hospital system a transaction for anesthesia indicates that there should be a transaction for an operation, and visa versa.

K. COMPLETENESS CHECK (BATCH)

Despite the fact that online system transactions are entered as they occur, the basic concept of batching is still valid. The difference is that in the online system the batch represents all of the input from *one user* for one application (over a period of time) and that the batch and batch totals are established after the fact rather than before data entry.

The primary purpose of batch controls in an online system, unlike that of the batch system, is proving that all of the documents intended for entry have been entered and providing both an audit trail and control information for subsequent processing. The batch tests are the same as the document tests for completeness except that they apply to batches rather than to documents.

L. SEQUENTIAL NUMBERING CHECKS

In many applications, documents and/or transactions have sequential numbers. Any transaction which is entered on paper should have a sequential document number and a sequential line number that shall be entered by the user. The system should check that the transactions entered are in sequence and that there are no gaps in the sequence. Sequential number checks provide a mechanism for identifying both operator and communication failures, as well as providing an audit trail.

M. PAGINATION

When entering documents which exceed twenty lines, divide the document into pages, and maintain individual page controls in addition to document controls. Page controls consist of counts of transacations, and totals of quantities and amounts. Page size should be at least three lines smaller than the total number of lines on the CRT screen in order to allow for display of the "page total" entry, including the computed totals.

Note: This will eliminate the problem of duplicating a page or item.

IV. VISUAL VERIFICATION

The online data entry system should always provide a visual confirmation at the operator's terminal and provide the operator with the opportunity to change the data. Visual verification shall be performed on a field-by-field basis, terminal and communications hardware permitting. This section should show all codes, expanded into full discriptions, e.g., the code "QQ18" should be displayed as "QQ18 - JOHN SMITH, INC."

Also, the system shall permit the user to "recall" and correct a transaction which has already been accepted as valid if the review and correction is to be accomplished. The user should be able to specify:

- Review Last - Recall the previous transaction.
- Review Page - Recall the entire page.
- Review Set - Recall the entire set.
- Review Batch - Recall the entire batch.

When a correction is made to a previously accepted transaction, the processing can be handled in one of two ways:

1. The original transaction can be reentered as originally keyed, and then the correction can be entered, or
2. Only the data fields in error can be altered.

The second approach is the one most commonly used in a batch system because of its ease for both programmer and user. The additional complexity required to delink and relink error records and the lack of documentation inherent in this approach, however, make it unacceptable in an online system (unless a separate Hold file is used).

Note: Error correction of previously entered transactions should be done on the delete and reenter basis, where the user must enter the transaction in its original, incorrect form, and then enter the correct transaction. The system should treat both of these as additions to the transaction file.

V. ERROR ANALYSIS

This section shall delineate various schemes to analyze the causes of errors, along with recommendations as to how to reduce error rates.

The online system can collect statistical data as to which operator is making errors and the type of errors being made. These records should be maintained for each operator and the performance of each user should be compared to all operators. Those operators which are exceeding the norms (that is, those with significantly higher rates of error than the average operator) shall be displayed on a special report, with a frequency count by type of error.

This report may then be used as a basis for additional training or counseling. The statistical output may also be used as an incentive for accuracy in data entry. Merit bonuses and raises may be provided to operators who have significantly lower error rates.

PRACTICE 0250
CURRENT SYSTEM SUMMARY

CONTENTS

I. INTRODUCTION

    A. GENERAL
    B. PURPOSE

II. USER INTERVIEW FORM

III. FLOWCHART AND PROCESSING NARRATIVE

IV. SOURCE DOCUMENTS DEFINITION

    A. ITEM NUMBER
    B. DOCUMENT NAME
    C. FORM NUMBER
    D. SOURCE DEPARTMENTS BY VOLUME
    E. KEY DATA ELEMENTS
    F. METHOD OF CONVERSION
    G. FREQUENCY OF INPUT
    H. ESTIMATE OF VOLUMES

V. OUTPUT REPORTS AND TRANSACTIONS
DEFINITION

    A. ITEM NUMBER
    B. OUTPUT NAME
    C. IDENTIFICATION
    D. TYPE OF OUTPUT
    E. CATEGORY
    F. ESTIMATE OF VOLUMES

G. OUTPUT SOURCE

H. OUTPUT DESCRIPTION

I. COMMENTS

VI. FILE DEFINITION

A. ITEM NUMBER

B. SOURCE

C. USERS

D. ESTIMATE OF VOLUMES

E. VOLATILITY

F. SEQUENCE OF DATA

G. PRIME DATA INFORMATION

H. DESCRIPTION AND COMMENTS

VII. PROCESSING OF VOLUMES AND
TIMING FACTORS

VIII. UTILIZATION AND COST OF PERSONNEL

IX. UTILIZATION AND COST OF COMPUTER
RESOURCES AND NON COMPUTER
EQUIPMENT

I. INTRODUCTION

A. GENERAL

This practice describes the information to be gathered during the study of the existing systems and includes a set of forms suitable for recording the necessary information.

B. PURPOSE

This practice outlines in detail the data to be collected as part of the study of the existing systems as well as the mechanics for collecting the data; mainly, user interview and existing documentation.

II. USER INTERVIEW FORM

User interviews and existing documentation are the two main sources of data used in examining present systems. The primary information source for manual processing and interfaces with the computer is provided by data collected from user interviews. Less than reliable documentation may result from incomplete entries. A knowledge of federal regulations may, however, serve to elucidate the needs of the user.

All key personnel to be interviewed may be identified using an organization chart. The kind of information to be gathered should be considered in structuring the interview. The interview should be scheduled well in advance and the interviewee should be notified about the kind of information that will be reviewed with him. If appropriate, the interviewee may be asked to provide documents.

SYSTEM:	DATE:	
SUBSYSTEM	INTERVIEWER:	
INTERVIEWEE:	TITLE:	DEPARTMENT:
JOB DESCRIPTION:		
TOPICS DISCUSSED:		
INPUT/OUTPUT		
INTERVIEWEE REQUIREMENTS AND PREFERENCES (Unmet needs)		

Figure 1.   User interview form.

Figure 1 is a sample form for use in collecting the data. Under the Topics Discussed heading, the following (at a minimum) should be included:

- How and where tasks are performed
- What functional task activities are performed

- Estimated number of people involved in each task.
- Amount of time required to accomplish each task.

When information from the data usage, flow, functions, and problems with the current system are summarized, this form will be a valuable source of information.

III. FLOWCHART AND PROCESSING NARRATIVE

A flowchart diagramming the manual procedures should be prepared as clearly as possible. It should identify all major flows of documents. Secondary and auxiliary functions should appear in a separate diagram. Computer processing functions should also appear in a separate diagram, expanding the function identified on the main diagram.

The main diagram should clearly identify the following:
- All major transactions and documents
- All functions performed—be explicit in describing the manual functions and computer functions, and show disposition of all documents entering a process
- Document used in each process
- Volume of documents entering and exiting a process
- Timing and scheduling for all processing functions

The narrative accompanying the flowcharts must be written in a clear fashion so that it is easily understood by users and analysts. It must be, of course, keyed to the flowcharts, using standard ANSI flowcharting symbols. To adequately explain functions and processes, charts and tables may be used. Timing estimates for real-time systems, file size, and other crucial parameters should also be provided.

IV. SOURCE DOCUMENTS DEFINITION

Documents that were originally used by the system to provide the basic input data (e.g., Invoice, Timeslip) are referred to as "source documents," and these must be identified and pertinent information entered in the form shown in Figure 2.

Instructions for filling in the form are as follows:

A. ITEM NUMBER:

A unique, sequentially assigned number to facilitate referencing to this form.

B. DOCUMENT NAME:

Self explanatory.

C. FORM NUMBER:

The number identifying the source document, if one is available.

SYSTEM:	Date:	Prepared by:

ITEM NO.:

DOCUMENT NAME:	FORM NO.:

SOURCE DEPT(S)/VOLUME(S):

KEY DATA ELEMENTS:

METHOD OF CONVERSION:	FREQUENCY OF INPUT:

ESTIMATE OF VOLUMES:

Period					
Minimum					
Average					
Maximun					

DISTRIBUTION OF DOCUMENT BY COPY/COLOR:

COMMENTS:

Figure 2. Description of input.

D. SOURCE DEPARTMENTS BY VOLUME:

List of departments responsible for preparing the source document and the volume prepared.

E. KEY DATA ELEMENTS:

A list of the primary data elements on the form.

F. METHOD OF CONVERSION:

How the source document is converted to machine-readable form (e.g., keypunching, key to tape, etc.).

G. FREQUENCY OF INPUT:

The cycle in which the source document is entered into the system (e.g., daily, weekly, as required, etc.).

H. ESTIMATE OF VOLUMES:

Minimum, average, and maximum volume estimates by period A period may be specified in terms of cycles (i.e., daily, weekly) or as a specific line period in order to account for peaks (i.e., 5th through 10th).

SYSTEM:		Date:	Prepared by:
ITEM NO.	DOCUMENT NAME	SOURCE DEPT(S)	FREQUENCY & VOLUME

Figure 3. Source document summary.

I.   COMMENTS:

Any additional information relevant to describing or clarifying the content, use, and purpose.

This information, collected during the interview with the user, may be recorded on the form at a later time. Samples of each source document must be examined and keyed to the form.

After all source documents are documented, a summary chart should be made, as in Figure 3.

SYSTEM:	Date:	Prepared by:

ITEM NO.:	OUTPUT NAME:	ID:

TYPE OF OUTPUT: --Report   --Transaction   --Visual Display

--Other _____

CATEGORY: --Summary --Detail --Exception --Error --Other

_____

ESTIMATE OF VOLUMES:

Period					
Minimum					
Average					
Maximum					

OUTPUT SOURCE:

OUTPUT DESCRIPTION:

COMMENTS:

Figure 4.   Description of output.

V. OUTPUT REPORTS AND TRANSACTIONS DEFINITION

Output reports, that is documents that are produced from manual or computer processing are first categorized, and then relevant information is recorded on the form shown in Figure 4. This information may be derived from current documentation or gathered during the interview with the user. Instructions for filling in the form are as follows:

A. ITEM NUMBER:

A unique, sequentially assigned number, to facilitate referencing to this form.

B. OUTPUT NAME:

Self-explanatory.

C. IDENTIFICATION:

The assigned identification code for the document, if applicable.

D. TYPE OF OUTPUT:

Self-explanatory.

E. CATEGORY:

Self-explanatory.

F. ESTIMATE OF VOLUMES:

Minimum, average, and maximum volume estimates by period. A period may be specified in terms of cycles (i.e., daily, weekly) or as a specific line period in order to account for peaks (i.e., 5th through 10th).

G. OUTPUT SOURCE:

The program or process responsible for generating the output defined.

H. OUTPUT DESCRIPTION:

A brief description of the content, purpose, and use of the output defined.

I. COMMENTS:

Any additional information relevant to describing or clarifying the production, use, content or purpose of this output.

After all outputs are documented, a summary chart should be made, as in Figure 5.

SYSTEM:			DATE:		Prepared by:	
ITEM NO.	OUTPUT NAME & ID	OUTPUT TYPE	OUTPUT CATEGORY	FREQUENCY	VOLUME (Pages or TXNS)

Figure 5. Output document summary.

VI. FILE DEFINITION

A file is defined as any collection of items of information related in form, purpose, and content. Both computer files and manual files should be documented on a form similar to that shown in Figure 6.

Instructions for filling in selected entries on the form are as follows:

A. ITEM NUMBER:

A unique, sequentially assigned number, to facilitate referencing to this form.

B. SOURCE:

Indicate where (i.e., subsystem, program, process) the file is initially created and where the last version of the file is created for this system.

SYSTEM:	Date:	Prepared by:

ITEM NO.	FILE NAME:	FILE ID:

FILE TYPE: --Manual   --Computer   Storage Media: _____

SOURCE:

USERS:

ESTIMATE OF VOLUMES:

Period				
Minimum				
Average				
Maximum				

VOLATILITY: ____No. Additions Per ___ ___ No. Deletions Per____

____No. Changes Per ____

SEQUENCE OF DATA:

PRIME DATA INFORMATION:

DESCRIPTION/COMMENTS:

Figure 6. Description of file usage.

C. USERS:

List all users (i.e., departments and subsystems) of the file.

D. ESTIMATE OF VOLUMES:

Provides minimum, average, and maximum volume estimates by period. A period may be specified in terms of cycles (i.e., 5th through 10th).

E. VOLATILITY:

. Indicate the number of additions, deletions, and changes made to the file within the most significant time period (i.e., daily, weekly, monthly).

F. SEQUENCE OF DATA:

If data is maintained sequentially or accessed randomly, specify the sequence in which the file is maintained.

G. PRIME DATA INFORMATION:

List the primary data elements maintained on the file.

H. DESCRIPTION AND COMMENTS:

Provide a brief description of the content, use, purpose and processing requirements for the file.

After the required information is documented, all files should be summarized, as in Figure 7.

SYSTEM:			Date:		Prepared By:		
ITEM NO.	FILE NAME/ID	FILE TYPE	SOURCE	STORAGE MEDIA	MONTHLY VOLUME EST.	
					Average	Peak

Figure 7. File usage summary.

VII. PROCESSING OF VOLUMES AND TIMING FACTORS

In the process of documenting current systems volume estimates for inputs, outputs, and files, the fluctuations of volume over time must be considered if the workflow is irregular and functional processing is periodic.

The following information must be presented:

- Input, output and file identification
- Functions of processing (e.g., keying, coding)
- Periods of processing (e.g., daily, weekly, monthly)
- Average and peak volume per period
- Time restrictions (e.g., "Keying must be completed by 9 p.m.")

Narrative explanations and graphs, which may be used to illustrate variations, should be presented. For further analysis, crucial controls and constraints should be given emphasis.

VIII. UTILIZATION AND COST OF PERSONNEL

The cost and number of personnel required for each function should be identified by personnel category. Full-time equivalent units may be used to record fractional personnel participation.

For each job category, a standard cost for each function should be derived from the following factors:

- Average salary (for that category)
- Fringe benefits (Average costs)
- Relevant overhead cost (e.g., work space, supplies, recruiting cost)

This information should be documented on a form similar to that shown in Figure 8. Instructions for filling in the form are as follows.

A. FUNCTION/PROCESS

A brief description of what the manual procedure involves.

B. CATEGORY:

Position responsible for the manual operation defined.

C. DEPARTMENT:

The area (i.e., department, section) of the subsystem in which the manual procedure is required.

D. STANDARD COST:

The derived standard cost for the job category described.

SYSTEM:					Date:					
SUBSYSTEM:					Prepared by:					

FUNCTION/ PROCESS	CATEGORY	DEPARTMENT	STANDARD COST	NO. OF PERSONNEL NEEDED			TOTAL COST		
				Period 1	Per. 2	Per. 3	Per. 1	Per. 2	Per. 3

Figure 8.   Personnel requirements and costs for manual procedures.

SYSTEM:

Date: Prepared by:

MONTHLY TOTALS

PROCESS/FUNCTION	ESTIMATED CPU TIME	ALLOCATED CPU COST	OTHER EQUIP. COST	NUMBER OF TERMINALS	COMMUNICATION/ TERMINAL COST	TOTAL COST
MONTHLY TOTALS						
YEARLY TOTALS						

Figure 9. Utilization and cost for computer and other equipment.

E. NUMBER OF PERSONNEL NEEDED:

The number of people needed to perform the described manual operation. The period will vary, depending on the frequency of operation. It may be, for example, daily, weekly, bi-weekly, monthly, yearly.

F. TOTAL COST:

The number of people needed for a period multiplied by the standard cost.

IX. UTILIZATION AND COST OF COMPUTER RESOURCES AND NON-COMPUTER EQUIPMENT

Both computer utilization and non-computer equipment must be identified by processing function, documented, and costed. Computer utilization reports are the best source of information for measuring computer utilization and costs. If these are unavailable, estimates of CPU time must be derived.

Non-computer equipment used by the system will include EAM equipment, copying machines, microfilm, and so forth. A separate category is terminal and communication resources.

For determining computer cost, the standard cost unit must define the allocated cost unit, which consists of: rental cost of CPU and peripheral equipment, the cost of the maximum number of operations personnel, and computer processing space and supplies.

To determine the cost of non-computer equipment, multiply the total monthly equipment cost times the percent of total time used for each function.

Associated line charges, communication equipment, and terminal lease and rental charges are among the communication and terminal cost.

Figure 9 illustrates how the utilization and cost of computer resources and equipment should be summarized.

X. OTHER FACTORS

Also to be documented are other important factors identified during the review, and any collected information vital for the analysis. "Important" factors may include the following:

- Constraints and controls
- Current system's impact and interface on other systems
- Implications for management
- Requirements for audit
- Requirements for projected growth or reduction
- Current system's economic evaluation

PRACTICE 0260
SYSTEM TEST PLAN

CONTENTS

I. INTRODUCTION

    A. GENERAL
    B. PURPOSE

II. TEST STRATEGY OVERVIEW

III. SYSTEM TEST PLAN

I. INTRODUCTION

A. GENERAL

This practice provides guidance on the creation of a test strategy to insure proper testing of the system. It also specifies the development of a System Test Plan (STP) to implement that strategy.

B. PURPOSE

This practice describes the type of test plan that shall be prepared for all major programming projects.

II. TEST STRATEGY OVERVIEW

Inadequate attention to testing a new system leads to undesirable consequences (e.g., an academic institution failed to properly test a registration program. It was believed that, because of the confusion, a number of students failed to register and had gone to other institutions instead. Also, it turned out that there were unnecessary billing errors in the accounting subsystem, leading to further lost revenue. Haphazard testing of new programs is a major cause of fiascos such as this.

This practice stresses two major points:

1. An overall *testing strategy* must be developed that describes the general approach to testing the individual components and the integrated system. This strategy includes but is not limited to:

A. The order of sequence in which sub-components of the system are to be tested (e.g., common subroutines, worker sub-programs, main programs, control logic within a function, overall transaction paths).

B. The major phases of testing that are to take place prior to operational release. For instance:

(1) Sub-program test with canned data.

(2) Program test with canned data.

(3) Control logic test within major functions.

(4) Control logic test by major transaction types.

(5) High volume test with test data generator.

(6) Single station test with live input.

(7) Multiple station test with live input.

(8) Trial period with organizational units.

C. The description of data base to be used in checking out the system.

D. The test data base to be used shall be described as follows:

(1) Source(s) of data

(2) Types of records

(3) Number of records

(4) Format of data

(5) Volume of data

(6) Data structures (indexes, keys)

III. SYSTEM TEST PLAN

A proper test of the system requires a formal test plan that specifies the purpose of *each* test in each test phase, identifies the components being tested during that test, and states the expected results. If automated aids are to be used, these should be indicated.

The test plan may include who will conduct the test, if persons other than the developer are going to conduct some of the tests.

B. SYSTEM TEST PLAN

Routines of an illustrative test plan are shown below:

Phase	Test No.	Purpose of Test	Modules Being Tested	Results
Progam checkout controlled data test	1	Check out standard edits or phone install TX	PROCALL	Error messages shall appear on screen
	2	Check out special edits on phone install TOLL TX	PROCALL TOLLCALL	
	3	Check out calculation of work performance breakdown	CALCWB	Printout of TX
Integration test	1	Check out the status settings or linkage records after spec-ified trans-action events		Selective memory dump
	2	Check out log-in routine, all terminals simultan-eously		See display panel
	3	Check out temporary SAVE		
	4	Check out system status display		See display panel

SERIES 0300

documentation aids

SHORT HIPO DOCUMENTATION GUIDELINE

CONTENTS

I.   INTRODUCTION

    A. GENERAL
    B. PURPOSE

II. INTRODUCTION TO HIPO

III. INTRODUCTION TO SHORT HIPO

IV. COMPONENTS OF HIPO/SHORT HIPO

    A. THE VISUAL TABLE OF CONTENTS
    B. THE OVERVIEW DIAGRAM
    C. THE DETAIL DIAGRAM
    D. THE EXTENDED DESCRIPTION
    E. DECISION TABLES AND/OR STRUCTURED
       FLOWCHARTS

V.   WHEN TO PREPARE SHORT HIPO/HIPO
    DOCUMENTATION

VI. STEP-BY-STEP PREPARATION OF
    SHORT HIPO/HIPO DIAGRAMS

VII. SHORT HIPY/HIPO AS A MANAGE-
    MENT AID

    A. CONTENT REVIEW
    B. CONSISTENCY REVIEW
    C. TECHNICAL ACCURACY REVIEW

D. FUNCTIONAL ACCURACY REVIEW
E. IMPLEMENTATION REVIEW

FIGURE 1: CASE MANAGEMENT SYSTEM VTOC
FIGURE 2: HIPO OVERVIEW DIAGRAM
FIGURE 3: SHORT HIPO OVERVIEW DIAGRAM
FIGURE 4: SHORT HIPO DETAIL DIAGRAM
FIGURE 5: DECISION TABLE

I. INTRODUCTION

A. GENERAL

This practice describes a shorthand method of using the Hierarchy plus Input-Process Output (HIPO) technique. It is a modification of the IBM HIPO technique, which simplifies the diagram preparation by eliminating much of the need for graphical presentation of the data and control flow.

Since HIPO only defines the processing logic, it is not a full set of documentation. The overall documentation content, organization, and format are prescribed in the System Development Cycle Documentation Guideline practice.

B. PURPOSE

This practice provides a brief explanation of HIPO and defines a specific short version of this technique.

II. INTRODUCTION TO HIPO

HIPO is a documentation technique which produces both system or program specifications and final documentation. It has long been recognized that the customary practice of not documenting a system or program until the end of the development cycle results in considerable extra effort. Documentation prepared at the end of the development phase often duplicates design specifications, and may result in documentation which does not accurately reflect the system or program being documented. The preparation of documentation prior to performing the work being documented is, and has always been, a desirable goal, but the number of changes in logic during the development effort generally make this goal unattainable.

HIPO is a documentation technique, which produces documentation suitable for use both as specifications and as the final documentation of a system or program. The basic premise of HIPO is to document what the system or program is to do, rather than how the tasks are to be done. Since the functions required to meet any specific goal do not change, except possibly in the method by which they are performed, the specification of the functions required to implement a system or program, and hence documentation which specifies *what* rather than *how,* will also not change. HIPO specifies a system or program in terms of what is to be done, rather than how it is to be done.

HIPO, as described in the IBM manual, *HIPO—A Design Aid and Documentation Technique,* GC20-1851, has two weaknesses:

1. It is inadequate in describing the logic of a system or program.

2. It overemphasizes graphic form at the expense of content.

HIPO's failings, in regard to describing logic, are based on the lack of any means within HIPO of describing control mechanisms, i.e., the conditions under which various processing steps will be executed. HIPO's failings in regard to overemphasizing graphics, at the expense of content, are based on the time required to prepare a finished HIPO diagram of the type illustrated in the manual referenced: i.e., approximately one hour per diagram.

III.   INTRODUCTION TO SHORT HIPO

An abbreviated form of HIPO, known as Short HIPO, used in conjunction with decision tables and/or structured flowcharts, can be used for system and program documentation. The use of full HIPO diagrams, of the nature described in the above referenced IBM manual, can then be restricted to graphic presentations and will not be used as internal documentation.

The Short HIPO diagrams contain all of the essential ingredients of HIPO; in fact, a HIPO diagram can be prepared from a Short HIPO diagram, without reference to any other documents, but it is designed to minimize the time spent in preparing the documentation. The use of decision tables and/or structured flowcharts provides a means of documenting the logic to the system or program. Decision tables are the preferred technique because:

1. They are readily understood by non-data processors,
2. They can be proven to be correct and complete, and
3. They permit rapid and ready identification of common processing functions.

This guideline describes the use of Short HIPO in conjunction with decision tables and provides guidance in the preparation of graphic presentations of HIPO.

IV.   COMPONENTS OF HIPO/SHORT HIPO

HIPO documentation consists of four types of components:
1. The Visual Table of Contents.

2. An Overview Diagram for each "non-bottom level" function described.
3. A Detail Diagram for each "bottom level" function described.
4. An Extended Description for each Overview Diagram and Detail Diagram requiring clarification.

Short HIPO documentation consists of five types of components; the four types used in HIPO listed above, plus:

5. A Decision Table and/or Structured Flowchart for each Overview Diagram and Detail Diagram whose logic requires definition.

A.   THE VISUAL TABLE OF CONTENTS

The Visual Table of Contents (VTOC) resembles an organization chart. Rather than depicting the hierarchy of job slots within an organization, the Visual Table of Contents depicts the hierarchy of functions within a system or program. Case Management System VTOC, shown in Figure 1, is a representative Visual Table of Contents. Each block:

- Corresponds to one function required to accomplish the ends of the system or program design.
- Is shown in its position in the hierarchy: i.e., it is connected to the one block at the immediately higher level to which it is a component, and is in turn connected to each of the blocks at the immediate lower level, which are components of it.
- Contains the name of the function it represents, and a unique identifying number which serves two purposes: it distinguishes between functions which bear the same name, and it serves as a "page number," locating the Overview Diagram or Detail Diagram which describes the function.

All documentation is to be located in "page number" sequence; therefore, in addition to providing the hierarchy of the system or program, the Visual Table of Contents serves as the table of contents for the documentation of the system.

B.   THE OVERVIEW DIAGRAM

The blocks on the Visual Table of Contents can be classified as to whether or not they have subordinate blocks. Any function block on the Visual Table of Contents, which has subordinate level blocks, is a "non-bottom level" function, while function blocks which do not have subordinate blocks are "bottom level" functions. An Overview Diagram is required for each "non-bottom level" function depicted on the Visual Table of Contents. The purpose of the Overview Diagram is to name the inputs, the lower level functions, and the outputs associated with a function. The Overview Diagram consists of three rectangular boxes, each of which encloses a columnar list. The

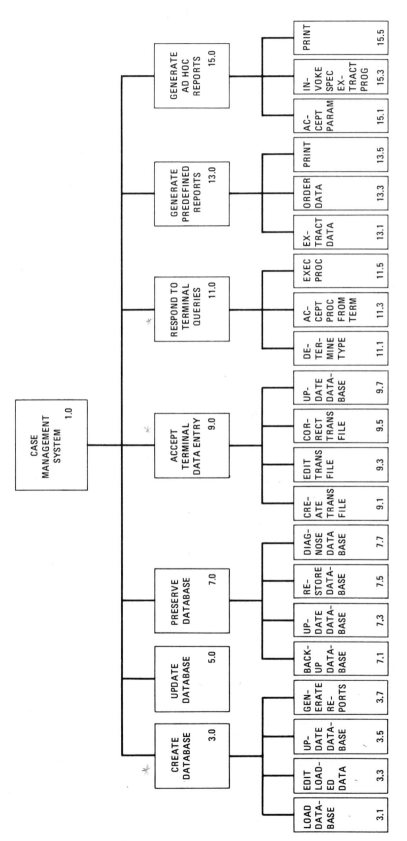

Figure 1. Case management system VTOC.

lefthand list names the inputs to the function, the middle list names the lower level functions required to accomplish this function, and the righthand list names the outputs from this function.

The HIPO Overview Diagrams (see Figure 2) require that inputs be grouped on approximately the same horizontal level as the functions, also called processess, to which they are input. Also, if more than one input is used by the process, all of the inputs for the process are to be enclosed in a box. Note that in Figure 2, the data base is input to several processes and is therefore included in several boxes. Arrows are drawn from each input or group of inputs to the edge of the box containing the processes to which the input(s) apply. Processes which share common input or produce common output may also be grouped together and enclosed in a box, as is the case for processes 13.0 and 15.0 in the illustration. Arrows are then drawn from the process to the diagramatic representation of the output of the process. Note that if the same output is produced by several processes, you may specify the output once, and connect several processes to it by arrows, as was done for processes 3.0, 5.0, and 7.0 in the illustration, each of which are connected to the output symbol for data base. The careful use of arrows, boxes within boxes, and graphic symbols, makes the HIPO Overview Diagram an ideal mechanism for explaining a system or program to a user, as well as a systems analyst or programmer.

The Short HIPO Overview Diagram conveys the same information as the HIPO Overview Diagram, but does so in a more concise form, at the expense of graphic notation. The problem with the graphic emphasis of the HIPO Overview Diagram is the time required to prepare each Overview Diagram. If it becomes necessary to prepare HIPO Overview Diagrams for graphic presentations, allow approximately one additional hour for each Overview Diagram so prepared.

As can be seen from Figure 3, the Short HIPO Overview Diagram omits the arrows, boxes within boxes, and the graphic symbols characteristic of the HIPO Overview Diagram. Also, each input is listed only one time regardless of how many processes into which it is input. The other noticeable difference is that the processes generating each output are specified by enclosing the process numbers in parentheses immediately following the output name.

The logic behind these variations is based on the fact that for each process named in an Overview Diagram, there is a lower level block, and either an Overview Diagram or Detail Diagram which more fully describes the process; therefore, there is no need to become too explicit at this higher level. If, for example, you are concerned with the process "Update Data Base," you will study the Overview Diagram for that function, rather than the diagram for the higher level function.

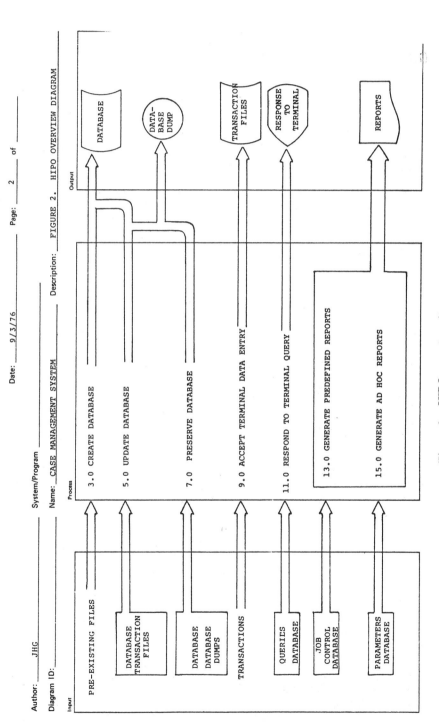

Figure 2. HIPO overview diagram.

Author: JHG

Diagram ID: 1.0

Date: 9/3/76

Page: _____ of _____

System/Program

Name: CASE MANAGEMENT SYSTEM

Description: FIGURE 3. SHORT HIPO OVERVIEW DIAGRAM

(0310-7)

Input

EXISTING FILES
DATABASE
TRANSACTION FILES
DATABASE DUMPS
TRANSACTIONS
QUERIES
JOB CONTROL
PARAMETERS

Process

3.0	CREATE DATABASE
5.0	UPDATE DATABASE
7.0	PRESERVE DATABASE
9.0	ACCEPT TERMINAL DATA
11.0	RESPOND TO TERMINAL QUERIES
13.0	GENERATE PREDEFINED REPORTS
15.0	GENERATE AD HOC REPORTS

Output

DATABASE (3.0, 5.0)
DATABASE DUMPS (7.0)
TRANSACTION FILES (9.0)
REPORTS (11.0, 13.0, 15.0)

Figure 3. Short HIPO overview diagram.

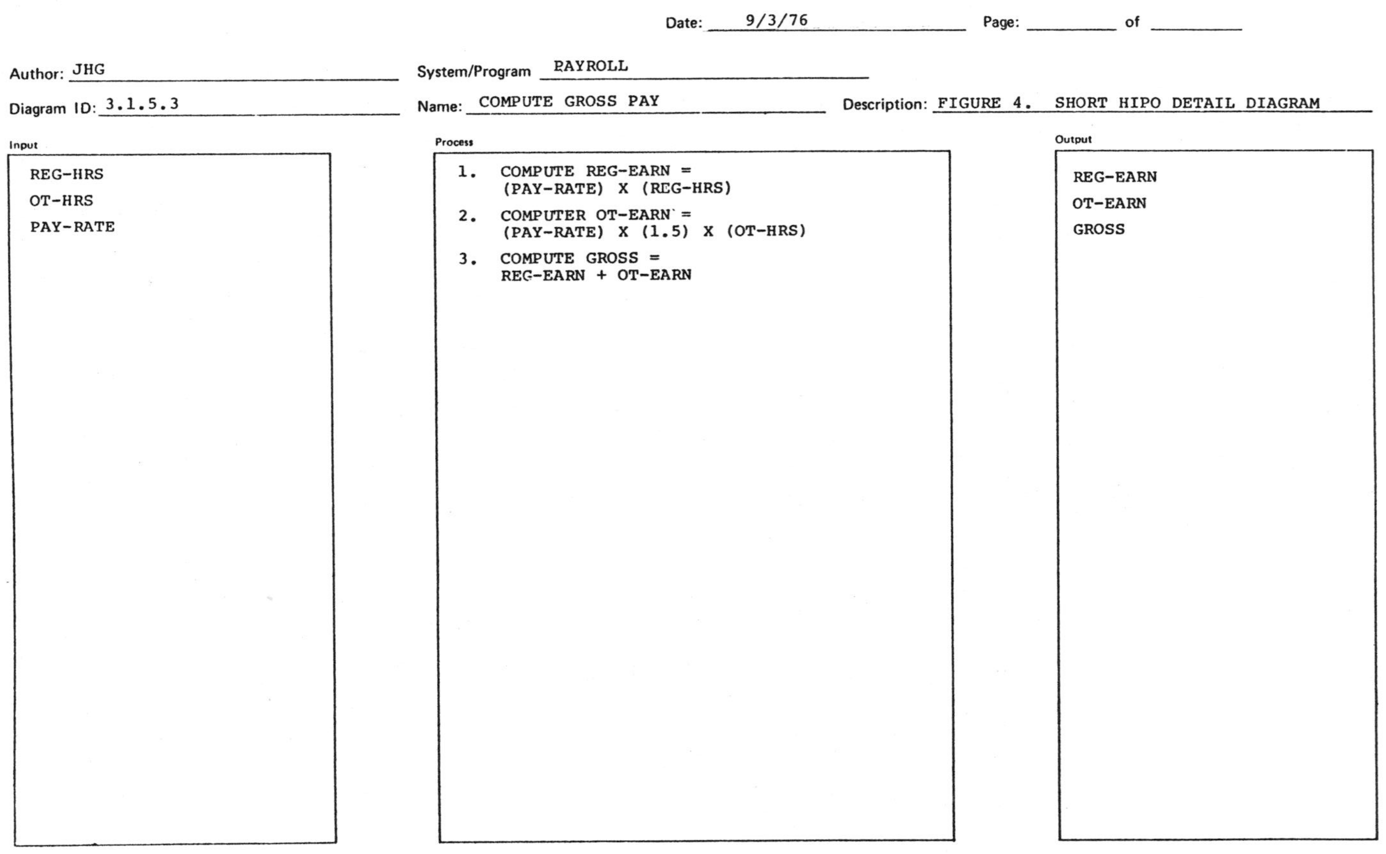

Author: JHG

Diagram ID: 3.1.5.3

System/Program   PAYROLL

Name: COMPUTE GROSS PAY

Date: 9/3/76

Page: _____   of _____

Description: FIGURE 4.   SHORT HIPO DETAIL DIAGRAM

Input

REG-HRS
OT-HRS
PAY-RATE

Process

1.   COMPUTE REG-EARN =
     (PAY-RATE) X (REG-HRS)

2.   COMPUTER OT-EARN =
     (PAY-RATE) X (1.5) X (OT-HRS)

3.   COMPUTE GROSS =
     REG-EARN + OT-EARN

Output

REG-EARN
OT-EARN
GROSS

Figure 4.   Short HIPO detail program.

C. THE DETAIL DIAGRAM

A Detail Diagram is required for each "bottom level" function depicted on the Visual Table of Contents. The Detail Diagram is identical in appearance to the Overview Diagram, and differs only in that it specifies that tasks, rather than lower level functions, be performed as the processes required, to produce the outputs associated with the function. Figure 4 is a typical Detail Diagram. Note that the inputs specified are field names, as are the outputs, rather than record names, and that the processes specified are elementary in nature.

D. THE EXTENDED DESCRIPTION

The Extended Description is used to supplement and clarify Overview Diagrams and Detail Diagrams where needed. For example if one of the processes specified is "validate transaction code," the Extended Description would be used to list the valid transaction codes. Other uses of the Extended Description include the specification of formulas used to compute output values, specification of the criteria which must be met before a calculation is performed or data is moved, and to convey any other required information not specified explicitly in the Overview or Detail Diagram with which the Extended Description is associated.

Care should be taken to avoid specifying logic in the Extended Description. The purpose of HIPO and Short HIPO is to specify *what* is to be done, not *how* it is to be done. The specification of "how to do it" should be left to the Decision Tables and/or Structured Flowcharts.

E. DECISION TABLES AND/OR STRUCTURED FLOWCHARTS

Because HIPO is unsuited for the specification of control, i.e., logic, it must be supplemented with techniques which are suitable for specifying logic. The conventional flowchart has proven unsatisfactory, primarily because it has too few constraints and is therefore ambiguous. The techniques used to describe logic should be highly constrained so that they are not ambiguous.

Two techniques which meet these qualifications are the Decision Table and the Structured Flowchart. The Decision Table is the preferred technique because it permits more precise specification of the logic involved, and because it permits rapid identification of common processing functions. Figure 5 is typical of the types of Decision Table which are to accompany Short HIPO documentation. In the table illustrated, the conditions required to determine the regular hours worked (REG-HRS) by an employee and the overtime hours worked (OT-HRS) are defined. There are two rules to follow:

1. Overtime is paid only to hourly employees.
2. Overtime is the number of hours worked in excess of 40.

```
    HIPO WORKSHEET
|                                                                          |
|  Author: JGH  System/Program:  Payroll     Date:09/03/76 Page: 1 of  1   |
|  Diagram ID: 3.1.5.1  Name: Det. Reg. & OT Hrs.  Descrip.: Decision Table |
|                                                                          |
|  HOURLY EMPLOYEE          ||  N | Y | Y |                                |
|  ------------------------ ||----|---|---|                                |
|  HRS-WRK > 40             ||  - | N | Y |                                |
|  ------------------------ ||----|---|---|                                |
|                           ||    |   |   |                                |
|  REG-HRS = 40             ||  x |   | x |                                |
|  ------------------------ ||----|---|---|                                |
|  REG-HRS = HRS-WRK        ||    | x |   |                                |
|  ------------------------ ||----|---|---|                                |
|  OT-HRS = 0               ||  x | x |   |                                |
|  ------------------------ ||----|---|---|                                |
|  OT-HRS = HRS-WRK - 40    ||    |   | x |                                |
|  ------------------------ ||----|---|---|                                |
|                           ||    |   |   |                                |
```

Figure 5. Decision table.

There are also two implicit assumptions:
   1. Salaried employees are always paid for 40 hours regardless of how many hours they actually work.
   2. All hours worked are to be classified as either regular or overtime.

If the designer is not familiar enough with the system to make implicit assumptions of this nature, no actions will be specified for conditions of whose effect the designer is uncertain. As a result the designer will be unable to identify specific conditions requiring additional investigation. The result is that all conditions will be investigated and that the resulting specification will be complete; i.e., accounts for all known conditions and prescribes actions for each set of known conditions.

The structured flowchart is a highly constrained variation of the conventional flowchart in which only four constructs are allowed. These constructs are:
   1. Sequence
   2. IF-THEN-ELSE
   3. DO-WHILE
   4. CASE

The sequence construct is used to depict processes in which no decisions occur. The IF-THEN-ELSE construct is used to depict processes in which an either/or decision is to be made. Then, on the decision, either one of two sub-processes is to be executed. The DO-WHILE (also the DO-UNTIL) construct is used to provide for looping or executing a process while (or until) a condition is met. The fourth construct, the CASE, is named for the PL/I CASE statement, which is similar to the COBOL GO TO DEPENDING. The use of the IF-THEN-ELSE and the CASE is constrained in that immediately after executing the selected process, control returns unconditionally to the next sequential construct in the Structured Flowchart.

It is recommended that the use of Structured Flowcharts be restricted to graphic demonstrations and not used as either systems or program documentation.

V. WHEN TO PREPARE SHORT HIPO/HIPO DOCUMENTATION

The use of Short HIPO/HIPO requires a different conceptual treatment of documentation and implementation than is customary. The customary treatment is to divide documentation into two categories:
1. Specifications documentation prepared before work is performed.
2. Final documentation prepared after work is complete.

Short HIPO/HIPO, when used in conjunction with decision tables, eliminates the need for the preparation of final documentation and produces specifications documentation which is also suitable for use as final documentation.

The preparation of Short HIPO/HIPO documentation begins with the investigative study of the proposed system and continues on a reiterative basis, through design and implementation of the system. At each step during the study, design, and implementation process, additional levels of Short HIPO/HIPO documentation are prepared to serve as the specifications for the design and implementation of the system.

The methodology to be followed is:
1. Prepare an Overview Diagram for the function.
2. Expand the Visual Table of Contents to reflect the functions identified in developing the Overview Diagram.
3. Reiterate.

The first step in documentation of a system or program is then to prepare the overall Overview Diagram (see Figure 3 for an example), which specifies as its functions the major components of the system or program being designed. The next step is to generate, using this data, the first level of hierarchy on the Visual Table of Contents. Next, for each process named in the Overview Diagram, prepare an Overview Diagram, and expand the Visual Table of Contents an additional level. When the point is reached where tasks rather than functions are being specified, Short HIPO/HIPO is complete.

The next step is to go back to the top level, and prepare Decision Tables for each Overview and Detail Diagram requiring an explanation of the logic. On completion of the Decision Tables, the design documentation for the system is complete and ready for review by the user.

Once the user has approved the system design, the individual programs are designed in much the same manner as the system. The most significant difference is that in addition to updating and expanding the Visual Table of Contents at each iteration, code is prepared and tested.   This overlapping of program design and implementation provides a means of limiting the effect of an error and assuring the elimination of logic errors before work proceeds.

VI.   STEP-BY-STEP PREPARATION OF SHORT HIPO/HIPO DIAGRAMS

A. Use the HIPO worksheet (Figure 2).
B. List all of the outputs of the functional process in ouput column of the form.   Use the file, report, and data item names that are standard for the system or program.
C. List all of the inputs that you know *are* required.
D. List any inputs that you think *may* be required.
E. List the steps of the functional process. If need be, prepare a decision table, to enable the identification of the processing steps.
F. Specify any intermediate outputs which are used only as input to subsequent processing in the same functional process.
G. Specify any tables or lists of valid codes, etc. on the HIPO Extended Description.
H. Delete any inputs which are not required.
The following apply only to formal HIPO diagrams:
I.   Connect corresponding inputs and processes with arrows.
J.   Connect corresponding processes and outputs with arrows.
K. Redraw the diagram with the inputs for a process step clustered and the outputs of each process step clustered in boxes.

VII.   SHORT HIPO/HIPO AS A MANAGEMENT AID

One of the most significant aspects of the use of Short HIPO/HIPO is that the diagrams become a management aid for use in the control of the project work.   Feedback, in the form of reviews of the Short HIPO/HIPO diagrams, provides the information that management needs to monitor both progress and accuracy of the development effort. The value of this feedback is greater than when using customary documentation techniques because it is available before considerable effort is expended doing something in an incorrect manner. This is because the Short HIPO/HIPO diagrams are available for review before they are implemented while when using customary documentation techniques, the feedback information is not available until after the work is performed.

A.   CONTENT REVIEW

The objective of the content review is to assure that Short HIPO/HIPO has been used to generate a truly hierarchical system or program design.   Only if the design is truly hierarchical in nature is it possible to determine if the design is complete, i.e., that the system or program, is implementated in accordance with the design, will indeed produce all of the required outputs, using only the specified inputs. There are three questions which must be satisfied when performing a content review:

1. Is the Visual Table of Contents a true hierarchy structure?
2. Is each block at one level of the diagram described by the lower level blocks for the block in question?
3. Are the inputs and outputs for each block a subset of the inputs and outputs for the next higher level block which is being described?

Unsatisfactory diagrams must be corrected before either design or implementation is allowed to proceed.

B.   CONSISTENCY REVIEW

The objective of the consistency review is to assure that the format of the Short HIPO/HIPO diagrams is consistent and that the notations, symbols, acronyms, etc. are consistent from one diagram to the next, throughout the entire system. In the case of HIPO, particular emphasis is placed on the consistent use of arrows, the grouping of inputs and outputs associated with the same process, and graphic symbols. This emphasis is based on the use of HIPO diagrams as presentation aids, rather than any added utility imparted to the diagrams. The questions which must be satisfied when performing a consistency review are:

1. Is the terminology consistent throughout?
2. Is the terminology understandable to the users of the documentation, i.e., if a design diagram subject to review or reference by the user of the system, have concepts been expressed in the terminology of the user department, rather than data processing?
3. Are file data items, report, and input names consistent throughout?
4. Are all acronyms and technical data processing terms defined in user terms?
5. Is each input directly traceable to either a raw input to the system or to the output of a function which is to be executed prior to the execution of the block in which the input is used?

Unsatisfactory answers to the first four questions dictate that the documentation be corrected before proceeding. Unsatisfactory answers to the fifth question require that the VTOC and the design be corrected before proceeding.

C.   TECHNICAL ACCURACY REVIEW

The objective of the technical accuracy review is to assure that the Short HIPO/HIPO documentation clearly describes a complete system or program. Note that this review does not prove that the system or program is functionally complete, i.e., that it will accomplish all of the objectives required to satisfy the user. It does mean that the system or program, as described, will successfully accomplish all of the objectives which have been included in the Short HIPO/HIPO diagrams. The questions to be answered are:

1. Are the outputs of each functional process clearly defined?
2. Based on the inputs to the process, the decision tables, and the extended description provided for the process, can each of the specified outputs be developed?
3. Based on the above, are any inputs and/or outputs omitted?
4. Is the process clearly described?

Unsatisfactory responses dictate that the documentation, or the design, be ammended, whichever is appropriate, before proceeding.

D. FUNCTIONAL ACCURACY REVIEW

The objective of the functional accuracy review is to assure that the system or program, as described, does in fact satisfy the requirements of the user. The functional accuracy review should be conducted by user personnel in conjunction with data processing personnel. The questions to be resolved are:

1. Are functions correctly stated in user terminology?
2. Has anything been added or omitted?
3. Are the inputs and outputs, at the user level, correctly specified?

Unsatisfactory answers to any of these questions dictate that the design be modified before proceeding.

E. IMPLEMENTATION REVIEW

One of the key differences in the technique described here, and customary techniques, is that implementation, i.e., coding performed in a hierarchical manner, can proceed in parallel with the design effort. As soon as the design has been reviewed and accepted, the coding of the accepted portions can be performed. As soon as the coding for one functional process is coded, it should be tested, independently of all other functional processes on the same level, and its operation verified. The inputs and outputs of the test should be reviewed to determine:

1. That the module accepts all specified inputs.
2. That any "unspecified" inputs are rejected.
3. That each input follows the correct path through the module of code.
4. That each of the specified outputs is correctly produced by the code.

These facts should be determined by comparing the inputs and outputs of the test to the Short HIPO/HIPO diagrams for the module. Any discrepancies require that the code be modified to produce the results specified in the Short HIPO/HIPO documentation.

PRACTICE 0320

DATA CORRELATION AND DOCUMENTATION SYSTEM

CONTENTS

I. INTRODUCTION

    A. GENERAL
    B. PURPOSE

II. DESCRIPTION OF DCD

    A. ANNOTATED SOURCE LISTING
    B. LAYOUT DOCUMENTATION
    C. DATA CORRELATION ALPHABETIC
       CROSS REFERENCE

III. USING DCD AS A PROGRAM DESIGN AID

    A. DCD OUTPUTS REQUIRED
    B. METHODOLOGY
    C. WHERE USED

IV. USING DCD AS A TEST AND
     DEBUGGING AID

    A. REQUIRED OUTPUTS
    B. METHODOLOGY

V. USING DCD OUTPUT AS DOCUMENTATION

    A. REQUIRED DCD OUTPUT
    B. METHODOLOGY

VI. USING DCD AS A MAINTENANCE AID

    A. REQUIRED DCD OUTPUTS
    B. METHODOLOGY

VII. USING DCD OUTPUT AS THE SOURCE OF
    DATA DICTIONARY INFORMATION

    A. REQUIRED DCD OUTPUT
    B. METHODOLOGY

VIII. OPERATING INSTRUCTIONS

    A. INDEPENDENT MODE
    B. COMPILE MODE
    C. GENERAL COMMENTS
    D. RETURN CODES

IX. SYMBOLIC PARAMETERS

X. SAMPLE JCL

XI. DCD MESSAGES

I. INTRODUCTION

A. GENERAL

This practice describes an automation aid for documenting individual COBOL programs. It is a standardized system for generating documentation of program logic and data format.

B. PURPOSE

The Data Correlation and Documentation (DCD) system establishes a standardized procedure to be used to document all programs written in COBOL.

II. DESCRIPTION OF DCD

The DCD system is a comprehensive automated programming and

documentation aid for COBOL source programs. DCD provides assistance in the development of programs, the program review process, debugging, and maintenance. In addition, the DCD output can serve as a significant part of the formal documentation of a program, and provides layout documentation which can be used to develop the manually maintained data dictionary.

DCD output is of three types:

- Annotated Source Listing
- Layout Documentation
- Data Correlation Alphabetic Cross Reference

A. ANNOTATED SOURCE LISTING

The annotated Source Listing is based on the customary COBOL source listing. In the event that more than one line of comment is required, additional lines, containing only the annotation, are generated. The annotation for DATA DIVISION entries specifies:

1. Each use of the data item by stating the operation performed, the statement number in the PROCEDURE DIVISION, and, if applicable, the statement number in the DATA DIVISION of the target or source data item.
2. Whether the data item has a special use, such as subscript or logic operator. If the data item is used as a subscript, the subscripted data item is named to facilitate cross reference.

The annotation for PROCEDURE DIVISION statement is quite different:

1. The statement numbers in the DATA DIVISION of each item referenced in the statement are specified.
2. If the statement is the target of a GO TO, or PERFORM, the statement numbers of each such GO TO or PERFORM are listed.
3. If the statement contains a GO TO or PERFORM, the statement number of the branch is listed, and if the branch is conditional, this is specified in the annotation. If the branch is a PERFORM, the statement number of the statement from which the return is made is also specified.

B. LAYOUT DOCUMENTATION

The Layout Documentation output generated by DCD provides a graphic description of each file, each record, and each 77 level data item in the program. An annotated table is generated for each file and for each record and 77 level data item defined in the working storage section of the program. The file tables have a heading section, describing the characteristics of the file, such as the FD name, blocking factor, label type, recording mode, etc. The annotation for the heading specifies the PROCEDURE DIVISION statements in which the file is opened, closed, and accessed.

The body section of the table contains entries for each data item. The COBOL level number and data item name are specified for all items. For the lowest level items in hierarchical structures, the length, data type, beginning position in the record, and ending position in the record are also specified. The annotation for the body section of the table specifies each reference and use of the item in the PROCEDURE DIVISION. This annotation is identical in nature to that appearing alongside DATA DIVISION entries in the Annotated Source Listing.

All entries in the Layout Documentation are keyed to the statement number used in the Annotated Source Listing.

C. DATA CORRELATION ALPHABETIC CROSS REFERENCE

The Date Correlation Alphabetic Cross Reference listing is the third output of the DCD. Arranged in alphabetic sequence, this report for each file, record, data item, literal, and figurative constant specifies the statement number in which the data is defined, and the name used in the program. In addition, each PROCEDURE DIVISION statement referencing the item is identified, and the action is fully described as the operation is specified, the name of the target/source field is specified, and the name of the paragraph in which the operation occurs is specified.

III. USING DCD AS A PROGRAM DESIGN AID

A. DCD OUTPUTS REQUIRED

1. Annotated Source Listing
2. Layout Documentation

B. METHODOLOGY

1. The annotation for the PROCEDURE DIVISION entry and exit points is traced to verify:
   a. Program logic flow
   b. Conditions under which code is to be executed.
   c. That switches and indicators, whose contents dictate execution flow, are initialized, set, and reset correctly.
   d. That data movement and computational operations are performed in the proper places in the program.
2. The Layout Documentation is used to verify:
   a. The correct specification of input and output records.
   b. That all required output fields are in fact created during program execution.
   c. That all required output fields are created from the correct sources, using the specified computations.

C. **WHERE USED**

1. The programmer shall use the DCD output as a means of desk checking program logic prior to testing.
2. Structured walk-through (peer group) members shall use the DCD output as a means of verifying the control logic of the program, and the conditions under which various outputs are generated.
3. Design review (inspection) members shall use the DCD output to verify control logic, and the conditions under which output is generated.

IV. USING DCD AS A TEST AND DEBUGGING AID

A. **REQUIRED OUTPUTS**

1. Annotated Source Listing
2. Layout Documentation
3. Data Correlation Alphabetical Cross Reference

B. **METHODOLOGY**

1. Determine scope of problem; e.g., applicable to all fields in a record type, applicable to one field of many in a record type, applicable to outputs for a specific input condition.
2. Use the Annotated Source Listing to find and identify logic problems.
3. Use the Cross Reference output to determine where field contents are modified, then verify both operations and the content of the operands used.
4. Use Layout Documentation to verify the format and content of all input files.
5. Check input fields for content values which are not expected, and therefore may result in deviation from the planned logic flow.

V. USING DCD OUTPUT AS DOCUMENTATION

A. **REQUIRED DCD OUTPUT**

1. Annotated Source Listing
2. Layout Documentation
3. Data Correlation Alphabetic Cross Reference

B. **METHODOLOGY**

1. Run DCD against the COBOL source which is turned over to operations.
2. File with other program documentation.

VI. USING DCD AS A MAINTENANCE AID

A. REQUIRED DCD OUTPUTS

1. Annotated Source Listing
2. Layout Documentation
3. Data Correlation Alphabetic Cross Reference

B. METHODOLOGY

1. Determine nature and scope of change; e.g., if a field is computed $y \times 3 - s^2$ and there is a modification to the formula used to compute "s" it would be necessary to determine where it is used, and to determine whether any other element of the formula is impacted.
2. If the change to a field is unconditional, identify each PROCEDURE DIVISION statement changing the field, using the Cross Reference, and modify each such statement.
3. If the change to a field is conditional, using the Annotated Source Listing and the Cross Reference, identify the PROCEDURE DIVISION statements affecting the field when the condition applies, and modify them.

VII. USING DCD OUTPUT AS THE SOURCE OF DATA DICTIONARY INFORMATION

A. REQURED DCD OUTPUT

1. Layout Documentation

B. METHODOLOGY

1. Associate the file name with the program FD name.
2. For each data dictionary entry, specify the program name, program FD name, and program data name.
3. Under the data name used in the program, if it differs from the standard name for the data item, make the following entry: Program name, program FD name, standard name for the data item.

VIII. OPERATING INSTRUCTIONS

The DCD system comprises a series of consecutively executed programs, which analyze a COBOL program, and generate up to three types of documentation as earlier described. DCD may be operated in either of two modes, independent or compile. Two PROCs are provided for this purpose.

A. INDEPENDENT MODE

The PROC for this mode is called DCDSRC. In this mode, DCD accepts as input a COBOL source program in sequential form. The JCL required to operate DCD in this mode is very simple. For example:

```
//   EXEC DCDSRC, options
//STEPLIB      DD     DSN=PSI.LIB,VOL=SER=FDS005,DISP=
   SHR,UNIT=3330
//DCDMAIN.COPYLIB DD    (Optional copy library)
//DCDMAIN.CD    DD    (source program)
```

B. COMPILE MODE

In this mode, input to DCD is the SYSPRINT output from the COBOL compile step. In this case, the SYSPRINT data set is redirected to temporary direct access storage, and used by the PROC,DCDCOMP, as input to DCD.
For example:

```
//   EXEC COBUC    (or COBUCL, COBUCLG, etc.)
//COB.SYSPRINT DD DSN=&&COMPLIST,DISP=(,PASS),
//   UNIT=SYSDA,SPACE=(1210,(500,50)),
//   DCB=(RECFM=FB,LRECL=121,BLKSIZE=1210)
//COB.SYSIN    DD    (source program)
//   EXEC    DCDCOMP,options
//STEPLIB    ,,,
```

This mode may also be invoked by using a combination compile/DCD PROC. (See sample JCL).

C. GENERAL COMMENTS

Options are specified by adding symbolic parameters to the EXEC statement for DCD. Options for the two PROCs are identical with the exception of the parameter, RESOLVE. This parameter is operable for DCDSRC only, and controls the resolution of COPY statements embedded in a COBOL source program. In the compile mode, all COPY statements are resolved by the compiler.

It should be noted that the PROC, DCDCOMP, contains an extra step, which will retrieve and print the compiler-generated source listing, in the event that DCD does not terminate normally. It should be noted further that the correctness of the DCD output is guaranteed only in the case of an error-free source program.

The symbolic parameter descriptions and examples of use on the following pages illustrate user options and JCL requirements for the two PROCs.

D. RETURN CODES

The DCD system is designed so that, when running in the compile mode (DCDCOMP), the user is assured of getting a printout of the input source program in the following cases:

    1. The compile step returns a code > 4.
    2. DCD fails to complete, e.g., due to insufficient core.
    3. The option SRCLIST was not specified.

If SRCLIST was requested, and the DCDMAIN step completes normally, the return code for DCDMAIN will be 001, and the second step will not execute.

IX. SYMBOLIC PARAMETERS

The following parameters are set to either "1" or "0" unless otherwise indicated.

Keyword	Use	Default *
ALLNAME=1	Adds all unused data names into the alphabetic cross reference listing.	Names left out.
LAYOUT=1	Requests the layout documentation.**	Report not produced.
LINECT=NN	Requests that NN lines be printed per page.	60 lines per page.
PRINT=X	SYSOUT Class for SYSOUT, SYSPRINT, ETC.	CLASS=A
REG=NNNK	Requests that a larger region or partition be used to process a larger program.	100K
RESOLVE=1	Resolve COPY statements in a source program.***	Resolve COPY statements.
SPACE=1	Specify this parameter in the JCL to leave a line space after the narrative for each data name in the source listing	Prints an asterisk (*) before the first line of the narrative for each data name.
SORTREG=nnnnnn	Establish region size for embedded SORT. Six numeric digits must be coded.	999999
SRCLIST=1	Requests the annotated source listing documentation (Procedure Analysis and Data Analysis).**	Report produced.

SUB=1	Requests that the usage of all subscripts be documented in the narrative beside the DATA DIVISION.	Subscript usage documented.
WORK=XXXXX	Unit designation for direct access work space.	SYSDA
AREF=1	Requests the alphabetic cross reference.**	Report not produced.

NOTE: * The default parameter will produce only the annotated source listing.

         ** At least one of the parameters (LAYOUT=1, AREF=1, or SRCLIST=1),
            must be specified to run DCD.

         *** Applicable for DCDSRC only.

X. SAMPLE JCL

A. DCDSRC

```
1.  //    EXEC    DCDSRC
    //STEPLIB    ,,,
    //DCDMAIN.COPYLIB  DD  DISP=SHR,DSN=USER.COPY-
    LIB
    //DCDMAIN.CD    DD  *
        (source deck)
```

In example (1), DCD will produce the source list only from a card deck resolving all COPY statements from the PDS,USER.COPYLIB.

```
2.  //    EXEC DCDSRC,LAYOUT=1,AREF=1,RESOLVE=0
    //STEPLIB    ,,,
    //DCDMAIN.CD    DD    DISP=SHR,DSN=USER.SRCLIB
    (MBR 1)
    //
```

In example (2), DCD will produce the outputs for SRCLIST,LAYOUT, and AREF for the program MBR1 which is a member of the PDS USER.SRCLIB. COPY statements, if any, are ignored.

B. DCDCOMP

```
1.  //    EXEC COBUCL
    //COB.SYSPRINT DD DSN=&&COMP LIST,DISP=(,PASS)
    //    UNIT=SYSDA,SPACE=(1210,(500,50)),
    //    DCB=(RECFM-FB,LRECL=121,BLKSIZE=1210)
    //COB.SYSIN DD DISP=SHR,DSN=USER,SRCLIB(PGM2)
    //    EXEC DCDCOMP,LAYOUT=1
    //STEPLIB    ,,,
```

Example (1) indicates that the source program, PGM2 in the PDS USER, SRCLIB will be compiled and linked. The subsequent execution of DCD will produce SRCLIST and LAYOUT. If DCD does not terminate normally, say some table size has been exceeded, the last step in DCDCOMP will produce the source listing output normally produced by the procedure COBUCL.

C.   COMBINATION COMPILE/DCD PROC

A special PROC may be set up to facilitate the use of DCD in the compile mode. The result is a combination of compilation, DCD and link edit steps. For example, to obtain a compilation, a DCD run and a linked module, one would code:

```
1.  //    EXEC COBUCLD,LAYOUT=1
    //COB.SYSIN DD DISP=SHR,DNS=USER.SRCLIB(PGM2)
    //
```

This example is exactly analogous to example (B-1). The user should check, before using, with the system's programming group to see that the PROC has been installed, and what name it has been given (COBUCLD is arbitrary).

XI. DCD MESSAGES

A.   'NOTE.   COMMUNICATION SECTION NOT SUPPORTED IN THIS RELEASE OF DCD.   PROCESSING FOR THIS SECTION WILL BE BYPASSED.'

This message is printed if a program being processed contains communication section code that is not currently supported by DCD. The communication section code is bypassed, and all normal program documentation is performed.

B.   'ONLY ONE PROGRAM MAY BE INPUT, SUBSEQUENT PROGRAM BYPASSED.'

This message appears if two programs are input to DCD; only one program at a time is acceptable.

C.   'NAME TABLE LIMIT EXCEEDED.   RUN TERMINATED.'

This message appears whenever an internal table limit is exceeded. Rerun the program with a larger region size.

D.   'MULTIPLE SOURCE FIELDS IN (data name) EXCEEDS MAXIMUM, CORRELATION TERMINATED AT 20.'

The maximum number of source fields in a single statement is limited by DCD to 20. The operations for those source fields in excess of 20 will not be documented.

E. 'MULTIPLE TARGET FIELDS IN (data name) EXCEEDS MAXIMUM, CORRELATION TERMINATED AT 20.'

The maximum number of target fields in a single statement is limited by DCD to 20. The operation of those target fields in excess of 20 will not be documented.

F. 'COPY MEMBER (xxxxxx) NOT FOUND. PROCESSING TERMINATED.'

The specified member cannot be found in the COPYLIB data set. Either re-run with RESOLVE=0 or specify correct COPYLIB.

G. 'COPYLIB DATA SET NOT FOUND. PROCESSING TERMINATED.'

The specified COPYLIB could not be found on the volume given on the DD card. Correct the DD card and re-run.

H. 'UNSUCCESSFUL READ FOR COPY MEMBER (xxxxxx). PROCESSING TERMINATED.'

An error occurred during the read of the COPYLIB. Correct and re-run DCD.

I. 'UNSUCCESSFUL READ FOR COPYLIB DIRECTORY. RUN TERMINATED.'

An error occurred during the read of the directory of COPYLIB. Correct and re-run DCD.

J. 'DSN FOR COPYLIB NOT SPECIFIED. PROCESSING TERMINATED.'

A data set name was not specified on the COPYLIB DD card. Modify the DD card and re-run DCD.

SERIES 0400

operations

PRACTICE 0410
JOB CONTROL LANGUAGE STANDARDS

CONTENTS

I. INTRODUCTION

    A. GENERAL
    B. PURPOSE

II. JOB CONTROL LANGUAGE

    A. FORMAT CONVENTIONS
    B. JOB STATEMENT
    C. EXEC STATEMENT
    D. DD STATEMENT
    E. OTHER JCL CONVENTIONS

III. JOB CONTROL LANGUAGE PROCEDURES

    A. LIBRARIES
    B. JCL HINTS
    C. FREQUENTLY USED PROCEDURES

FIGURE 1: AN EXAMPLE OF RANDOM JCL

I. INTRODUCTION

A. GENERAL

This practice serves as the primary guide to preparing JCL for production systems. It is organized in the following three basic areas:

1. The general purpose of JCL standards and how they should be employed.

133

2. Detailed usage information for the primary JCL statements.

3. Usage information on system libraries and catalogued procedures, and hints on JCL usage.

Recognizing that the best standard is one which is complied with more easily than it is ignored. This practice has been reduced to only the most commonly employed JCL conventions. It assumes a high degree of familiarity with JCL, and with the concepts of operating systems.

B. PURPOSE

The purpose of this practice is to guide the programmer in preparing JCL for production systems. Production systems are those systems which generally adhere to four criteria. They are:

1. Designed and tested to a given specification.

2. Documented to the organization's standards.

3. Customer-approved prior to "live" implementation.

4. Placed under appropriate security, to insure subsequent changes and modifications are made in a controlled manner.

Programmers should be constantly aware that JCL can greatly affect the operating efficiency of OS. In preparing JCL they should try to:

1. Smooth the flow of the job stream by eliminating unnecessary operator intervention.

2. Eliminate time-consuming operations wherever possible.

3. Insure conflicts do not occur between data sets.

4. Make the job device independent where possible.

5. Include realistic space allocations.

6. Keep the environment for the job "clean" by deleting or removing unnecessary data sets.

II. JOB CONTROL LANGUAGE CONVENTIONS

A. FORMAT CONVENTIONS

The ability to quickly read and refer to JCL parameters is an important part of preparing good JCL. For this reason, all JCL will adhere to the following coding conventions:

1. // in Columns 1 and 2.

2. Name field begins in Column 3.

3. The operation begins in Column 12 for PROC and EXEC statements, or in Column 13 for DD statements.

4. Only one parameter per line is permitted. All operands must begin in Column 16, except the first operand on a PROC or EXEC statement having an eight-character name, which must be as coded in Column 17.

5. Successive statements are separated by a blank comment line.

6. All production catalogued procedures or similar data sets (e.g.,

WYLBUR, TSO) will contain the procedure name, programmer or developer, and function in the format shown in the example in Figure 1.

HASP control and OSI job cards need not conform to these conventions.

```
//AAABB JOB (9999,B01,10,20),'BB.TEST JCL RUN.SP'
/*ROUTE PRINT  REMOTE81
//*********************************************************
//*
//* PROCEDURE NAME
//* TEST JCL EXAMPLE
//*
//*
//* PROGRAMMER
//* SYNOPTIC SYSTEMS, INC.
//*
//* FUNCTION
//* SAMPLE JCL PROCEDURE TO DISPLAY FORMATTING
//* CONVENTIONS
//*
//* RESTART PROCEDURE
//* JOB MAY BE RESTARTED AT STEP BBPRO004
//*********************************************************
//BBPRO001 EXEC PGM=IEHLIST,
//              REGION=60K,
//              TIME=(,30)
//*
//SYSPRINT  DD SYSOUT=A
//*
//SYSIN     DD DSN=CN999.AAA.BB.TESTFIL.SPEC,
//             DISP=SHR,
//             VOL=SER=12345
//*
//SYSOUT    DD DSN=CN9999.AAA.BB.NEWTEST.SPEC,
//             DISP=(NEW,CATLG,DELETE),
//             VOL=SER=12345
```

Figure 1.   An example of random JCL adhering to the FTC format convention.

B. JOB STATEMENT

All jobs will adhere to the following conventions:

1. Job name—will consist of five user-specified characters in the following format:

   //iiizz

   Where:

   iii = Assigned timesharing system initials

   zz = The system job code assigned by the systems development group.

2. Account number – as required.

3. Bin or HASP terminal number – as required.

4. Maximum CPU time in minutes – *required on all jobs submitted.* Do not let the system default to the 30 minute time limit. Use an adequate (but not *excessive*) amount to prevent 322 abends.

5. Maximum lines printed – as required.

6. Maximum number of cards punched — should be noted as zero. Generally speaking, it is a policy *not* to utilize card media for input or output in production systems. Exceptions to this standard should be specifically approved.
7. Special forms — as required.
8. Number of times output is to be printed — as required.
9. Lines per page — as required.
10. Programmer name — adheres to the format shown in Figure 1. Briefly, it consists of no more than twenty characters which describe the basic function of the job and its frequency. This information may be entered free form.

Other special conventions which apply to the JOB statement are:

1. Do not use REGION parameter in the JOB statement. Include this in the EXEC statement.
2. RESTART = STEPNAME.PROCSTEPNAME. Restart capability must be specified on all jobs which involve more than three steps. This facility allows a job that is resubmitted for execution to be restarted at a particular step. All steps preceding the restart step are not executed. (Note that the restart step and subsequent steps cannot employ backward references, and that references to generation data sets, created in earlier steps, are also altered.) Before including this parameter, refer to the appropriate job control language reference manual for specific implementation data. The RESTART parameter should be placed as a comment card within the particular jobstream, or catalogued procedure to which it applies. Restart instructions should also be included in the operator documentation.
3. The following parameters are generally not allowed for normal processing. Usage of these parameters must be specifically approved prior to inclusion in production systems. The parameters are:
   a. PRTY
   b. ROLL
   c. MSGCLASS
   d. RD
   e. TYPRUN

C. EXEC STATEMENT

1. *General*

   The EXEC statement is the first JCL statement of each step in a job. The main function of the EXEC statement is to identify the program to be executed or the procedure to be used. Additional parameters may be used to allow the user to supply information to the application program through the PARM parameter, processing options may be specified through the

COND and TIME parameters, and main storage information through the REGION parameter. The format of the EXEC statement is illustrated below:

```
//Stepname    EXEC      Operand "1",
//                      Operand "2",
//
//
```

Generally it is recommended that only one parameter per line be employed on this statement.

2. *Stepname*

   Each step in a production system will have an eight character step name which carries the system code as the first two characters and is followed by a free form description of the function of the step.

3. *Execute Statement Operands*

   Operands specified on the EXEC statement control the programs or procedures to be executed. All application programs (as opposed to IBM utilities and other special programs) must be stored in user-defined libraries (referenced by JOBLIB or STEPLIB parameters). More information on these libraries can be found in Section IIIA. Specific operands for the EXEC statement and related standards are discussed below:

   a. *PGM* — Names the program to be executed in this job step. All program names will consist of seven characters and will adhere to the following conventions:

      PGM=aabccdd where:
         a = System code
         b = Language
         c = Function
         d = Sequence number
      See also Figure 1.

   b. *Procedure Name* — Specifies the procedure to be executed. This parameter consists of an eight-character name. Format conventions can be found in Figure 1.

   c. *COND* — Tests condition codes of previous steps to determine if the current step is to be executed. If used, insure the conditions for this parameter are well documented as comment statements in the procedure or job stream JCL.

   d. *PARM* — May contain up to 100 characters of data for interfaces with application programs. Make sure this parameter is well documented in the JCL, if used.

   e. *REGION=nnnK* — Used to specify the amount of core for this step. *All* special allocations for core should be made via this parameter on the EXEC statement, as opposed to the job statement.

f. *TIME=(minutes, seconds)* - Used to specify a given maximum CPU time for a given step. The following parameters are prohibited for use via the EXEC statement:

a. ACT
b. ROLL
c. DPRTY
d. RD

D. DD STATEMENT

1. *General*

The DD statement describes the characteristics of the data sets and indicates their location to the application program. Virtually all jobs require DD statements, since every program must have an input data set, or an output data set.

Only the programmer can fully determine the parameters necessary to adequately process the data sets which are required by the application programs. Since it is difficult to establish rigid standards in this area, the material in this section should serve as a guide in formulating the parameters for placement on the DD statement.

2. *Standards and Guidelines for DD Statement Parameters*

The notes and comments listed in this section for DD parameters are meant to augment or clarify their usage with regard to FTC applications. They are not meant to replace information contained in the IBM JCL manuals.

a. DSNAME = or DNS = Names the data set. Do not omit this parameter or use backward references. All data set names should follow standard naming conventions. Temporary data sets will use the "&&" prefix.

b. DISP = Specifies the disposition of the data set. Where possible, use all three parameters; i.e., DISP = (NEW, KEEP, DELETE), to prevent unnecessary placement of the name in the VTOC for jobs which abnormally terminate.

c. UNIT = Specifies device type.

d. VOLUME = or VOL = Identifies the volume on which the data resides.

e. LABEL = Describes the type of labels. The standard for this parameter will be

		standard IBM labels on all data sets generated by the systems.
f.	SYSOUT =	Routes a data set through the output stream.
g.	*	Indicates a data set is in the input stream. This should not be used except for routine compiles and tests.
h.	DATA =	Indicates input stream contains JCL to be treated as data.
i.	SPACE =	Requests space on a direct access device. (It does not apply to tape.) Space allocations first should be reasonable. Space allocations should also contain both primary and secondary allocations. (There may be rare circumstances when it is permissible to request everything primary to preclude abends.) Also, RLSE should be specified to insure all unused space is released.
j.	DCB =	Specifies particular data attributes.
k.	SEP =	Requests that the data be assigned a separate channel from the ones assigned to earlier data sets.
l.	AFF =	Requests the same channel as a data set defined on a previous DD statement. (See Section IIIB concerning use of this parameter).
m.	DUMMY =	Indicates that all I/O operations are to be bypassed for this data set. To be used *only* for test purposes.
n.	DSNAME =	Postpones definition of a data set.

E. OTHER JCL CONVENTIONS

1. *Use of Generation Data Sets*

A generation data set is one of a collection of historically related, catalogued data sets known as a "generation data group." The system keeps track of these data sets in chronological order, to make their access by production programs easier.

A complete explanation of generation data sets and their use can be found in the *IBM System/360 Operating System: Job Control Language Reference Manual.* To briefly summarize, they can be created, or retrieved, by identifying the generation data group name in the DSNAME parameter, and following the group name with the relative sequence number, or generation number. For example, DSNAME=MAST(-3), refers to the third oldest version of the data set MAST. Based on how the exact generation definition is performed, up to 255 different generation data sets can be "tracked" by the system.

2. *Retention of Data Sets*

The parameters specified for the use of generation data sets will, of course, be impacted by the retention requirements imposed on the data sets themselves. As a *minimum*, production systems should be designed with a minimum of a 120-day back-up period in mind. That is, it should be possible to completely recover from any software or hardware error up to a 120-day period after the occurrence of that error, provided notification is given. It should be noted, however, that this is a minimum requirement and that all retention periods must be approved by both the person or office responsible for the data and/or other appropriate personnel or authorities.

III. JOB CONTROL LANGUAGE PROCEDURES

A. LIBRARIES

Production systems will utilize three basic types of libraries; the *source statement library* will contain a copy of the latest source code for the system; the *load module library* will contain the latest load modules; and the *catalogued procedure library* will contain the latest version of the system procedures. Normally, each major application area will have these libraries available for inclusion of new source code and procedures. The security of these libraries will be dependent upon the particular requirements of the application being developed. Conventional security, unless otherwise specified, will consist of logging all changes to the libraries and maintaining back-up copies of the libraries.

Creation and maintenance of these libraries can be accomplished by using the standard IBM utility programs. For the most part IEBUPDTE will be used. This program requires the use of six control statements. These statements, and their function, are explained below:

Statement	*Function*
1. JOB	Initiates the job.
2. EXEC	Specifies the program to be executed (PGM=IEBUPDATE) and certain parameter information (PARM=...) depending on the particular program option desired.
3. SYSPRINT DD	Data set used for message, or lists.

		Normally, this will be coded as SYSOUT=A.
4.	SYSUT1 DD	The input (old master) data set.
5.	SYSUT2 DD	The new, or output, data set.
6.	SYSIN DD	The control data set. Often these instructions will reside in the input stream.

IEBUPDTE is a relatively easy program to use. The examples provided in the subsequent sections depict the normal source statements used to:

1. Create a library.
2. Change a particular member in a library.

The reader is cautioned to always refer to IBM publication GC-28-6586-13, *Utilities*, for complete information regarding the use of this program and utilities in general. Like any program which has many options, use of incorrect parameters can do significant damage to the data sets.

1. An Example of Creating a Library

    A partitioned library is to be created in this example. The input data is contained solely in the control data set.

    ```
    //UPDATE      JOB    099770, JOHN DOE
    //            EXEC  PGM=IEBUPDATE, PARM=NEW
    //SYSPRINT    DD     SYSOUT=A
    //SYSUT2      DD     DSNAME=OUTLIB, UNIT=3330,
                         DISP=(NEW,KEEP),
    //VOLUME=SER=123456, SPACE=(TRK,(100,,10)),
    //DCB=(RECFM=F, LRECL=80, BLKSIZE=80)
    //SYSIN       DD     DATA
    ./           ADD    NAME=MEMB1,LEVEL=00,
                         SOURCE=0, LIST=ALL
    ```

    (Data statements, sequence number in columns 73 through 80.)

    ```
    /*           ENDUP
    ```

    The control statements are discussed below:

    a. SYSUT2 DD defines the new partitioned master OUTLIB. Enough space is allocated to allow for subsequent modifications, without creating a new master data set.

    b. SYSIN DD defines the control data set. The data set contains the utility control statements and the data to be placed as a member in the output partitioned data set.

    c. The ADD Function statements indicate that subsequent Data statements are to be placed as members in the output partitioned data set. The ADD Function statement specifies a member name for subsequent data and indicates that the member is to be listed in the message data set.

2. *An Example of Updating a Library*

In this example, the existing data set, PDS, is to be updated with new records and renumbered.

```
//UPDATE        JOB    099770, JOHN DOE
//              EXEC  PGM=IEBUPDTE, PARM=MOD
//SYSPRINT      DD    SYSOUT=A
//SYSUT1        DD    DSNAME=PDS, UNIT=3330,
                      DISP=(OLD, KEEP),
//VOLUME=SER=123456
//SYSIN         DD    *
./             CHANGE  NAME=MODMEMB,LIST=ALL,
                       UPDATE=INPLACE
./             NUMBER  SEQ1=ALL,NEW1=10,INCR=5
(Data statement 1, sequence number 00000020)
(Data statement 2, sequence number 00000035)
/*
```

The control statements are discussed below:

a. SYSUT1 DD defines the data set that is to be updated in place. (Note that the member name need not be specified in the DD statement.)

b. SYSIN DD defines the control data set.

c. The CHANGE Function statement indicates the name of the member to be updated and specifies the UPDATE= INPLACE operation. The entire member is to be listed in the message data set.

d. The NUMBER Detail statement indicates that the entire member is to be renumbered, and specifies the first sequence number to be assigned and the increment value for successive sequence numbers.

e. The Data statements replace existing logical records having sequence numbers of 20 and 35.

B.   JCL HINTS

As programmers become more familiar with JCL and the conventions for particular machines, or data centers, they encounter certain practices which increase system thruput and often make systems more reliable and easier to maintain. An attempt has been made in this section to make a brief list of some of these practices. This list can be expanded as more shortcuts and efficiencies are developed.

1. Any procedure utilizing a small fixed input (for example, a member of a partitioned data set) must have comment cards that show exactly what is being input through that DDNAME, immediately following that DD card.

2. Procs will not contain a default for PRINTER. INSTEAD, use 'SYSOUT=A.'

3. The following card will be in every step, of every procedure:
    //SYSUDUMP DD SYSOUT=A

4. All input disk files will specify 'DISP=SHR.' All load libraries will *ALWAYS* specify 'DISP=SHR.'

5. If temporary data sets are to be put on specific disk packs, with the idea of passing them to subsequent steps, a permanent DSNAME (see 7 below) should be used when creating them. As the first step of the proc, run IEHPROGM to scratch and uncatalog the temporary data sets. The reasons for scratching them at the beginning, as opposed to the end of the job, are:

    a. If the job abnormally terminates, the last step (the one that scratches) would not have run, so the data sets would still be there. They would have to be scratched before re-starting, or else a duplicate DSNAME could appear.

    b. If the job runs successfully, a restart (if necessary) is much easier.

    c. The likelihood of getting the requested disk space on a specific pack is increased if data sets have just been scratched.

6. A DSNAME should not be used if temporary data sets are to be put on specific disk packs, to be deleted at the end of the step. If the system goes down, in this case, the data set most likely would not be deleted, as desired.

7. When permanent DSNAME'S are used for any reason, they must be absolutely unique. Index levels should be created, or existing ones used, to qualify the DSNAME.

8. Specify COND=EVEN, or variations thereof (for example, 'COND= (EVEN,(0,LT))'), for all steps that should execute regardless of abends from previous steps.

    All steps of a procedure that execute programs from private load libraries will have a STEPLIB card.

9. Data sets that are input and catalogued will supply the minimum information only—usually just the DSN and DISP parameter. Instead of, (for example):
    //MS DD DSN=A.B.C,DISP=SHR,UNIT=3330,VOL=SER=003135,
    //   DCB=(RECFM=F,LRECL=300, BLKSIZE=300)
    Code:
    //MS DD DSN=A.B.C,DISP=SHR

10. At many computer centers, tape units and disk drives allocated for a job step cannot total more than a fixed number. If more units are needed than are permitted in any given step, utilize the 'UNIT=AFF=' parameter. Also, to reduce costs, utilize this parameter whenever possible.

    If a DD card is in a step for the sole purpose of doing a volume refer-back to that DDNAME, a unit should not be allocated (tape) to that DDNAME. For example:

```
//DDIN          DD      UNIT=160BPI
//DDDUMMY       DD      UNIT=(1600BPI,,DEFER)
//DDIDIOT       DD      UNIT=(1600BPI,,DEFER)
```

requires allocation of three tape units. To reduce allocation to only one tape unit, code:

```
//DDIN          DD      UNIT=1600BPI
//DDDUMMY       DD      UNIT=AFF=DDIN
//DDIDIOT       DD      UNIT=AFF=DDIN
```

11. Region sizes should be as large as that step will ever need. For example, REGION=174K should not be used if that step will never need more than 100K. Supplying large regions to steps that do not require them will greatly increase costs. For user programs, 10K over what is required to allow for a SYSUDUMP and expansion room is sufficient.

C. FREQUENTLY USED PROCEDURES

Members of the Systems Analysis and Programming Section should file copies of general catalogued procedures, which are frequently used in the back of this practice for easy reference.

PRACTICE 0420

PRODUCTION CONTROL RUN BOOK

CONTENTS

I. INTRODUCTION

    A. GENERAL

    B. PURPOSE

II. RUN BOOK PREPARATION

    A. SYSTEM OVERVIEW

    B. SYSTEM SCHEDULE

    C. SYSTEM INPUTS

    D. SYSTEM OUTPUTS

    E. SYSTEM DATA FILES

    F. JOB OPERATING INSTRUCTIONS

I. INTRODUCTION

A. GENERAL

This practice contains a standard for preparing system documentation. It defines a standard set of information to be provided on each input data file and output used in the system. The job instructions needed to set up and run the job are also provided. The systems designer should follow a general format of this standard, adding additional information and instruction needed for a particular system.

B. PURPOSE

This practice defines the general format and content of the minimum documentation needed to run the system, and it is the responsibility of the systems designer to provide all additional documentation needed for normal operation, including handling of common abends..

II. RUN BOOK PREPARATION

Run books will be contained in three-ring binders and organized under
the following dividers:
A. SYSTEM OVERVIEW
B. SYSTEM SCHEDULE
C. SYSTEM INPUTS
D. SYSTEM OUTPUTS
E. SYSTEM DATA FILES
F. JOB OPERATING INSTRUCTIONS
Special forms are provided for B through F.

  Below is a description of the information to be contained in each of
the above-named dividers.

A. SYSTEM OVERVIEW

1. *System Narrative*
    Narrative description of the system. Describe the purpose of
    the system, major components, input data sources, utilization
    of outputs, and included references to any associated or inter-
    facing systems.
2. *System Flowchart*
    Flow all steps (machine and procedural). For all files and pro-
    grams, show full descriptive name as well as the abbreviated
    name used in the JCL.
3. *Special Requirements*
    List all special resources, if any, required to operate the system
    in terms of:
    (a) Manpower—i.e., operators, programmers, etc.
    (b) Software—such as type operating system, special compilers,
        or software packages.
    (c) Hardware—type hardware required to run the system.
    (d) Other - clerical support, data preparation, etc.
    If there are no special requirements, then indicate "None".

B. SYSTEM SCHEDULE

A master schedule shall be prepared on the form provided that shows job
identification, information, and run frequency.

C. SYSTEM INPUTS

Complete the following list of information for *each* system input:
1. NAME: Give full name of source document.
2. PURPOSE (Optional):   Describe the purpose of the input
                              in relation to the system.
3. SEQUENCE (Optional):   Give the sequence of the source

documents, and state whether or not the sequence must be retained during processing.

4.	FREQUENCY:	How often is the input processed?
5.	VOLUME:	State the volume of the input for each processing period.
6.	DISPOSITION:	Give the disposition of the input document after processing.
7.	RETENTION PERIOD:	How long should the input be retained after processing?
8.	PROGRAM(S) THAT PROCESS THE INPUT:	List name(s) here.
9.	JOB(S) THAT PROCESS THE INPUT	List name(s) here.
10.	FILE DSN OR DD:	Name of automated file created by the input.
11.	TRANSACTION TYPE:	Give the unique ID assigned to the input for program processing.
12.	INPUT FORMAT:	Use a separate sheet.
13.	SAMPLE SOURCE DOCUMENT	Use a separate sheet.

D. SYSTEM OUTPUTS

Complete the following list of information for *each* system output:

1.	NAME:	Give full name of output listing.
2.	PURPOSE:	Describe the use or function of the output.
3.	FORM:	List the type of form on which the output is printed (i.e., standard 11 x 14 2 part).
4.	SEQUENCE:	Give the sequence of the output (i.e., alpha by case name within state).
5.	FREQUENCY:	How often the output is produced (daily, weekly, as required, etc.)
6.	VOLUME:	The approximate number of pages that will be produced by the output.
7.	RETENTION PERIOD:	How long the output should be retained.
8.	PROGRAM/JOB THAT PRODUCES THE OUTPUT:	List the program or job steps here.
9.	DISTRIBUTION LIST:	List all users who receive output, and number of copies.

10.   SAMPLE OUTPUT: Use separate form.

E. SYSTEM DATA FILES:

Complete the following information for all files created or used by the system:

1.	FILE NAME:	Give full descriptive name of data file.
2.	DATA SET NAME:	DSN used in automated file labels. Should conform to defined DSN standards.
3.	FILE ID:	List the ID that is used in the JCL for this file. (See Job Control Language Standards.)
4.	PURPOSE:	Describe the data in the file and its use.
5.	MEDIA:	How is the file stored—tape, disk, cards, etc.
6.	FILE ORGANIZATION:	Sequential, random, ISAM.
7.	RECORDING FORMAT:	Fixed, variable.
8.	FILE SEQUENCE:	Sequential, indexed, random.
9.	RECORD LENGTH:	Specify number of characters in record.
10.	BLOCKING FACTOR:	Specify number of records per block.
11.	STORAGE REQUIREMENT:	Amount of disk space, number of tapes, etc.
12.	RETENTION:	List all retention requirements, both current and archival.
13.	PROGRAMS/JOBS:	List all programs or job steps that use the file.
14.	FILE FORMAT:	Use separate sheet.

F. JOB OPERATING INSTRUCTIONS

Prepare a set of instructions for *each* job in the system.

1.	JOB NAME:	Give full descriptive name of job.
2.	JOB ID:	ID used in Job Card in JCL.
3.	PURPOSE:	Describe purpose of the job.
4.	SCHEDULE:	When should the job be run? Be sure that this agrees with System Schedule.
5.	JOB SETUP:	Describe all the factors that must be present to run job.
	a. Input:	List file DSN of all inputs, and note

	b. Output:	any special handling, plus any JCL changes required. List file DSN of all outputs, and note any special handling, plus any JCL changes required.
6.	CONTROL TOTAL CHECKS:	Explain any control totals and how they are to be checked. As a minimum, the control totals should contain:

a. Number of transactions input to the job.
b. Number of records on input master.
c. Number of add records processed.
d. Number of delete records processed.
e. Number of records on output master.
f. Number of change records processed.
g. Number of invalid transactions, by category:
    − Adds
    − Deletes
    − Changes

7.	JCL RETENTION:	State how long JCL listing should be retained.
8.	ABEND MESSAGES:	Explain any program-generated ABEND messages and action required by production control.
9.	RESTART INSTRUCTIONS:	Define restart instructions for each job step within the job.
10.	PRINTING:	Provide alignment instructions on a sample output. Provide carriage tape if other than standard.
11.	JOB FLOWCHART:	Provide a flowchart of all I/O, data files, and programs, with any accompanying special instruction, if not shown in system flowchart.
12.	JOB CONTROL LANGUAGE LISTING (Catalogued)	Provide 80/80 listing of catalogued JCL.
13.	JOB CONTROL LANGUAGE LISTING (Run)	Provide 80/80 listing, or run JCL used, to initiate catalogued JCL. Indicate any changes that must be made by production control prior to each run.

TERMINAL OPERATOR'S MANUAL

CONTENTS

I. INTRODUCTION

    A. GENERAL
    B. PURPOSE

II. TERMINAL OPERATION

III. SIGN-ON, SIGN-OFF PROCEDURES

IV. SPECIAL FUNCTION COMMANDS

V. SPECIAL FUNCTION KEYS

VI. DIALOGUE FORMAT RULES

VII. TROUBLE-SHOOTING PROCEDURES

VIII. APPLICATION PROCEDURES

IX. ERROR MESSAGES

X. MANUAL FORMAT AND ORGANIZATION

FIGURE 1: SAMPLE SIGN-ON PROCEDURES
FIGURE 2: SAMPLE SIGN-OFF PROCEDURES
FIGURE 3: DEFINE COMMAND
FIGURE 4: KEYBOARD DESCRIPTION

FIGURE 5:   A TYPICAL TERMINAL OPERATOR
             PROCEDURE
FIGURE 6:   TERMINAL OPERATOR MANUAL—
             TABLE OF CONTENTS

I. INTRODUCTION

A. GENERAL

The terminal operator documentation must be comprehensive, clear, and easy to use. The instructions in this practice differ from conventional computer documentation in that they are often used by personnel who know nothing about data processing.

B. PURPOSE

The manual should contain all instructions which operators will require to use the system without referring to any other document. Specific topics to include are discussed in the following sections:
- Terminal operations
- Sign-on, sign-off procedures
- Special function commands
- Special function keys
- Dialogue format rules
- Trouble-shooting procedures
- Error messages
- Application procedures

II. TERMINAL OPERATIONS

The following items are to be included in this section of the manual:
- A diagram of the terminal, showing all switches and dials to be used by the terminal operator, should appear at the beginning of this section; e.g., the start switch, data error status light, and screen controls.
- A brief explanation of the use of the various terminal controls; e.g., the transmission mode switch must be set in the half duplex mode.
- A diagram to explain special terminal keys. A special numeric pad for computation, special function keys for performing editing operations, etc., are examples.
- An explanation of all keyboard functions that differ from the standard typewriter; e.g., the HOME key, when depressed, returns the cursor to the upper leftmost position on the screen.

III. SIGN-ON, SIGN-OFF PROCEDURES

This section contains a simple explanation of the sign-on procedure by which the operator may initiate a conversation. A careful distinction will be made between information to be entered by the operator, and information that the operator will receive. Show operator-entered information in lower case, and computer-generated information in upper case.

The description will include the procedures for establishing the connection with the computer; (e.g., dial the computer's number and depress the data button on the dataset). A sample sign-on procedure is shown in Figure 1. The procedures in the illustration contain actions to be taken when a problem is encountered.

```
Once the connection has been made with the resident computer and
the terminal keyboard is unlocked, the operator can sign on the
desired file.  A sample sign-on sequence is as follows:

        Operator:     sl/terms

        Computer:     YOUR NAME IS...

After the terminal prints:  'YOUR NAME IS...,' the next line of print
will be:

              PLEASE ENTER TERMINAL NUMBER

The number to be entered will be printed on a sticker located on
the front of the terminal.  If the number is incorrectly entered,
this message will be printed:

              ENTER NUMBER OF STICKER

If three tries at entering either the sign-on number or the terminal
number have failed, users will receive:

        *** *** *** *** ***  SIGN ON AGAIN

and other users will receive:

              RE-DIAL PHONE TO SIGN ON AGAIN

If the operator makes an error in the sign-on procedure--that is,
he uses a file name or identification number improperly, forgets
the file name, forgets to put the letter "s" in front of his number,
etc.--the computer types one of the following messages:

              FILE NAME ERROR
              LINE IS SIGNED OFF

              NUMBER ERROR
              LINE IS SIGNED OFF?

              NUMBER NOT ALPHABETIC
              LINE IS SIGNED OFF

              ADVISE SUPERVISOR xxxxxx-yy
              NOT IN FILE

              ERROR IN SIGN-ON NUMBER xxxxx
              REATTEMPT SIGN-ON

              ERROR IN FILE NAME
              REATTEMPT SIGN-ON
```

Figure 1. Sample sign-on procedures.

The sign-off procedures will contain an explanation of what the system does if the operator signs off in the middle of a transaction; e.g., midway into filling out an order form, or in the middle of a training course. (Will the operator be able to resume the transaction at the point at which it was interrupted?)

If the system itself can automatically sign off users, an explanation of the circumstances under which this will happen and the messages the operator will receive, must be given. A sample sign-off procedure is given in Figure 2.

If the system itself can sign off users, an explanation of the circumstances, and the messages the operator will receive, must be given.

```
Whenever the computer is waiting for an input from the terminal,
the user can use the sign-off command if he wishes.  A typical
sequence is:

        Computer:    WHAT IS THE PROPER ORDER NUMBER?

        User:        sign off (RETURN KEY)

        Computer:    LINE IS SIGNED OFF

The user's progress--his location within the entry at sign-off,
and other needed data--is kept.  This is necessary because the
user will continue at a later time.  When he next signs on, this
data is examined by the computer, and the file is reinstated at
the point where the user left off.
```

Figure 2.   Sample sign-off procedures.

IV. SPECIAL FUNCTION COMMANDS

The operator must be given a concise explanation of the purpose of the command, the command format, and arguments. The manual will contain a "layman's" explanation of the condition under which the command is to be used. Also, the sequence of computer and operator actions must be clearly presented. These two points are illustrated in Figure 3, which is a tutorial course for medical students.

Command descriptions shall contain a full explanation of the actions resulting from the use of that command. If several commands or function keys have associated use, the manual shall so indicate. As example is:

SAVE-Command

SAVE a transaction for up to 24 hours on the HOLD-FOR-CORRECTION file. (The RETRIEVE command is used to reactivate the transaction).

V. SPECIAL FUNCTION KEYS

An essential aspect of making the terminal operator's manual effective is a description of keyboard operations. While this information will

```
The define capability allows students to request definitions from
the computer.  Whenever the system is waiting for a response the
user may enter the word "define" followed by a space and then the
word he wishes defined.  An example is:

    define anticoagulant (RETURN KEY)

The program will give the definition and then return to poll the
student for his answer.  For example:

        Should the patient be treated...
          (computer type out; wait for
           student response)

        Define anticoagulant (RETURN KEY)
          (student request for help)

        An anticoagulant is...
          (response from dictionary;
           wait for student response)

        Antibiotic (RETURN KEY)
          (student enters answer to
           the question)
```

Figure 3.   Define command.

become second nature to an experienced operator, a new operator
will find it most helpful. Each special key should be fully explained.
An illustration of a keyboard description is shown in Figure 4.

VI. DIALOGUE FORMAT RULES

The principal purpose of this section is for the operator to learn the
rules, and to serve as a reference when the computer rejects an input
as unrecognizable. Distinction shall be made between punctuation
that is required, and punctuation that is optional, and is needed only
for easy reading comprehension. Syntactical rules shall be illustrated
with example screen output, including the message that would be
given for various types of rule violations.

VII. TROUBLE-SHOOTING PROCEDURES

In many situations terminal malfunctions cannot be readily explained.
This section of the manual explains to the operator, in a non-technical
language, the common causes of typical problems:
- Keyboard locks (will not accept input) after a system crash.
- Output messages are scrambled because of data transmission
  problems.
- Operator is cut off in the middle of transaction because the
  central system has an accidental disconnect problem.
- Operator looses screen display when he hits the NEXT key
  twice.

Control Keys

1. *Carriage Return*—The carriage return (CR) key causes the cursor to be positioned in the first column of the row immediately following the row in which the cursor is located. If the cursor is on row 30, rows 2 through 30 roll up one row, row 30 is erased, and the cursor moves to row 30, column one.

2. *Backspace*—The backspace key causes the cursor to move one location to the left and erase the character at the new cursor position. If the cursor is in column one, it will not move.

3. *Cursor Up* (   )—The cursor up key causes the cursor to move up one row on the VDU. It stays in the same column in which it is currently located. If the cursor is in row one, it does not move.

Special Function Keys

1. The LINE/LINE (Insert/Delete Line)—The LINE/LINE key is used to role text up or down the VDU allowing the deletion or the insertion of a line of data. When the unshifted LINE/LINE key is pressed, all data lines from and including the one where the cursor is presently located to the bottom of the VDU, are rolled down one line. Data on the bottom line is lost (rolled off the VDU) and the line the cursor is on is erased. The cursor does not move. This allows for the insertion of a line of data. When the shifted LINE/LINE key is pressed, the line the cursor is presently on is erased, and all data lines from the next line to the bottom of the VDU are rolled up one line. The bottom line is erased. The cursor does not move. This deletes the line the cursor is on and closes the gap.

2. CHR/CHR (Insert/Delete Character)—The CHR/CHR is used in conjunction with the cursor to perform editing on the display. It is doubly encoded.

    The unshifted CHR/CHR key moves all characters from, and including, the cursor position to the end of the line one character position to the right. The character in the last column is lost (shifted off of the display). The character position at the cursor location is erased. The cursor does not move.

    The shifted CHR/CHR key moves all characters from, and including, the cursor position to the end of the line one character position to the left. The original character at the cursor location is lost, i.e., replaced by the character immediately to its right.

Figure 4.   Keyboard description (selected samples).

- Portions of display output are cut off because the screen is improperly focussed.

VIII. APPLICATION PROCEDURES

This section contains procedures for performing the application functions; editing, updating, inquiry, etc. Each procedure should be shown on a separate page so that once the operator determines what is to be done, he will not inadvertently drift into some other procedure. A typical procedure is shown in Figure 5. The important aspect of the illustration is the detailed explanation of each step in the procedure.

Entering A Regular Order

1. Enter the order date in the form month/day/year (mm/dd/yy).

   The computer will reject a date if the year is not the current one, the date is later than today's date, or the date is more than five days earlier than the current date. If the date is rejected make the proper correction and reenter the date.

2. Enter the salesman number including the check digit.

   Salesman number will be rejected if either the check digit is wrong or if there is no such salesman. The computer will display "BAD CHECK DIGIT" or "NO SUCH NUMBER."

   If "BAD CHECK DIGIT" is displayed verify the number against the master list of salesman numbers in Appendix A and enter the correct number for the salesman.

   If "NO SUCH NUMBER" is displayed use the same procedure as above.

3. Enter the customer number including check digit.

   Customer number will be rejected if either the check digit is incorrect or if there is no such number.

   If "BAD CHECK DIGIT" is displayed verify the number against the master list of customer numbers in Appendix B and enter the correct number for the customer.

   If "NO SUCH NUMBER" is displayed first follow the procedure above, and if the customer is not listed enter "CANCEL" to cancel out the transaction and follow the procedure to set up a new customer and then enter this order.

4. Enter our order number.

5. Enter the customer's purchase order number.

   If there is no purchase order number enter the word "NONE."

6. Enter the requested shipping date in the form month/day/year.

   If no shipping data has been requested enter the word "NONE."

7. Enter the means of shipping the order.

   a. If we are the ship and the customer has specified speed, enter "FASTEST," other wise enter "CHEAPEST."

   b. If the customer is to pick up at the warehouse specify "OWN."

   c. If the customer has specified a particular carrier enter the carrier number.

8. Enter any special terms that the salesman has specified on the order.

9. For each item ordered:

   a. Enter the quantity ordered.

   b. Enter the item code including check digit.

   If "BAD CHECK DIGIT" is displayed verify the item number against the master price list and enter the correct number for the item.

   If "NO SUCH NUMBER" is displayed follow the procedure above, and if the item cannot be located in the price list notify the salesman. Enter the remaining items on the order.

   c. Enter the selling price of the item:

   If "PRICE ERROR" is displayed notify the salesman. Enter the remaining items on the order.

Figure 5.   A typical terminal operator procedure.

Notifying the Salesman

Fill out a salesman notification of order form.

BE SURE TO SPECIFY THE ORDER NUMBER.

Enter each item code that is in error and cleck off the proper box.

Figure 5.   (Cont.)

IX. ERROR MESSAGES

Error messages and an explanation are normally shown in a separate section of an application document. This standard requires that messages to be shown in the context of their normal occurrence

I.	Terminal-related procedure	
	A. Starting the terminal up in the morning	1
	B. Shutting the terminal down at the end of the day	2
	C. What to do if the terminal won't work	3
	D. Sign-on procedure	4
	E. Sign-off procedure	5
II.	Payroll-related procedures	
	A. Setting up a new employee on the system	9
	B. Changing the employee personnel record	11
	C. Entering time worked	14
	D. Entering requests for vacation pay, advances, etc.	15
	E. Terminating an employee	16
III.	Order Entry-related procedures	
	A. Setting up a new customer in the system	18
	B. Entering a regular order	19
	C. Entering a return memo (where salesman has picked up goods)	20
	D. Entering a pick up for return memo	21
	E. Establishing a shipping priority	22
	F. Checking the status of an order	23
	G. Changing and correcting orders already in the system	24
IV.	Grammatical Rules Appendix A--Error Messages	25
V.	Special Control Commands	25
VI.	Trouble-Shooting Procedure	30

Figure 6.   Terminal operator manual—table of contents.

during a discussion of procedures such as sign-on, operator commands, dialogue rules, application procedures, etc. The message below would be shown in the update procedure section.

35 disc address NNNN invalid.	The data base key has generated an address outside the file limits. The key may be invalid.

The operator's manual will contain an appendix, listing error messages, their ID, and an explanation.

X. MANUAL FORMAT AND ORGANIZATION

The manual should be designed as a convenient reference document. A small three-ring binder should be used; this allows the operator to keep it on the console along with the source documents.

A sample table of contents for a terminal operator's manual is shown in Figure 6. The information in the manual is organized into logical groupings. Housekeeping functions in terminal operation are in one section. The manual should have a special column which contains references to other pages in the manual that have related procedures. The manual should make liberal use of reference sheets since operators will use these for quick reference, and may wish to post them near the terminal. The manual itself will be used to look up answers to questions that arise during the interaction.

SERIES 0500

data base

PRACTICE 0510

DATA BASE ADMINISTRATOR

CONTENTS

I. INTRODUCTION

    A. GENERAL
    B. PURPOSE

II. FUNCTIONS OF THE DBA

III. SYSTEM ORGANIZATION

IV. SYSTEM MONITORING

V. SYSTEM REORGANIZATION

VI. RECOMMENDED DATA BASE ADMINISTRATOR POSITION DESCRIPTION

FIGURE 1: ALLOCATION OF THE DBA WORKLOAD
FIGURE 2: SAMPLE DATA BASE STRUCTURE DIAGRAM FOR A HYPOTHETICAL SYSTEM
FIGURE 3: SAMPLE DATA ELEMENT DESIGN FORM

I. INTRODUCTION

A. GENERAL

The Data Base Administrator (DBA) is an individual whose prime responsibility is to design and manage data base applications. The DBA acts as an interface between the systems analysts, who represent the end user, and the ADP technical operational personnel, who represent the computer resource for the organization. The major responsibilities of the DBA is to design and implement the data base, to establish procedures for accessing the data base, and to coordinate opportunities for data sharing. To this end, the DBA must possess a thorough understanding of software technology, including data base management systems as well as access methods and storage devices.

This practice depicts the full range of the DBA function. It is, however, unrealistic to assume that this function would be totally implemented based on resources presently available. Most organizations have found it advantageous to let this function develop gradually since it often counters more traditional approaches to data processing management.

B. PURPOSE

This practice defines the duties and responsibilities of the Data Base Administrator. In particular, it describes his duties pertaining to system organization, monitoring, and reorganization.

II.   FUNCTIONS OF THE DBA

The DBA performs functions in three primary areas: system organization, system monitoring, and system reorganization. System organization tasks are design-oriented activities, monitoring tasks are involved with "fine tuning" the data base, and system reorganization deals with environmental considerations, such as storage media, etc.

When the DBA serves as an organizer or designer, the individual will coordinate with the project leader, or systems analyst, in either designing a new data base, or modifying an existing one. The DBA will provide guidance in the practical considerations of data base design, such as naming conventions, storage media, data structures, and access methods. He will also deal with the finer details of the data base management system. The latter will include such items as the security system, audit system, and data dictionary standards.

System monitoring activities encompass such duties as being the custodian of the organization's automated data in the data base. The DBA interprets and ensures that all management policies on data copying, removal, and destruction are carried out. The DBA may choose to organize user groups. Through these groups the DBA may make known requirements for the administration of data standards, security systems, hardware, software, and other criteria for assurance of proper data base control. The DBA also monitors such items as CPU time, response time, and other production statistics, to ensure that all software is operating effectively.

System reorganization is primarily oriented toward maintenance of the data base and related software. The DBA will be responsible for reassigning data bases to different media, restructuring various data bases, removal of "dead" records and files, regenerating data base software, and installing periodic upgrades and software "fixes".

The allocation of time spent in these functional areas will vary significantly, depending on the organization. Figure 1 shows a reasonable amount of time to be allocated for the DBA resource to perform each function.

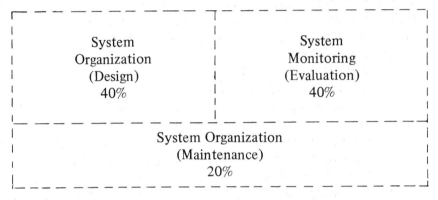

Figure 1.   Allocation of the DBA workload.

III. SYSTEM ORGANIZATION

One of the strongest justifications for a data base management system is, that it allows sharing of data, thereby reducing the need for maintaining redundant files. Optimizing a given data base for only one particular application often reduces the potential savings as other applications are implemented. The DBA must be charged with consolidation of varying user viewpoints, to ensure that the design accommodates the entire organization, and not just a single application. Resolution of these difficulties may involve the DBA developing policies which are based on both the technical merits of the data base management system, and the more human aspects of the organization.

Through participation in design, the DBA becomes familiar with the whole data base, the data structures required by application programs, and the storage structure. Design also includes search strategies and access methods, file membership rules, and record relationships.

It is during the design stage that rules can best be developed to constrain data base access. These rules would lay the foundation for resolution of future conflicts relative to shared usage. By introducing these rules during early development, problems involving concurrent updates or resource allocation conflicts may possibly be averted. These access constraints should be considered for all source and object programs under the DBA's jurisdiction.

Penetration, unauthorized update or copying, inadvertent disclosure, and removal or destruction of data can cause problems. Therefore, the DBA must specify the level of security required for various data bases (and segments therein) along with the level of access that a data user really needs.

The actual design of a data base requires that both the DBA and the systems analyst communicate their requirements in a precise, efficient manner. In order to place a degree of formality upon this process, several procedural guidelines have been outlined, along with some aids which may prove beneficial to both the DBA and the systems analyst during the design phase. The steps and products required as part of system organization are:

1. THE DBA WILL PLAN THE DESIGN OF THE PHYSICAL AND LOGICAL DATA BASE STRUCTURES. Prior to the release of a general system design, the systems analyst will submit to the DBA a structure diagram of the proposed data base (those unfamiliar with data base structure diagrams should refer to *An Introduction to Data Base Design* by John K. Lyon (New York: Wiley Inter-Science, 1971). This is a graphical representation of the logical organization of a data base. It specifies the relationships of records within, and between, files, much in the same manner as a high-level program flowchart indicates the interaction of procedures.

   There are two basic elements used to build a structure diagram. These are the rectangle and the arrow. The rectangle indicates the presence of entities; i.e., a group of things which are logically similar. The arrow represents the relationship between two or more entities. The structure chart below depicts a possible design for a skills data base.

```
 ------------     Skill      ----------     Operator    ----------
|            |     List      |          |     List      |          |
| EMPLOYEE   |-----------> | SKILL    |------------> | MACHINE  |
|            |               |          |               |          |
 ------------               ----------               ----------
```

   - Any EMPLOYEE may possess any number of SKILLS.
   - Any one MACHINE may be related to any number of persons who are skilled in its use.
   - A specific SKILL can, and must, be related to one, and only one, employee and to one, and only one, machine. (Under this data base schema, duplicate skills will appear in the data base.)
   - The arrow joining the EMPLOYEE and SKILL represents, collectively, all of the individual sets of SKILLS possessed by each employee.

- The arrow joining MACHINE and SKILL represents, collectively, all of the individual sets of SKILLS "owned" by each MACHINE.

In addition to specifying the proposed entities and their relationships, the analyst should also provide estimates for the number of occurrences ("records") for each entity, primary and secondary access keys, and any other pertinent information. An example of a hypothetical structure chart is shown in Figure 2.

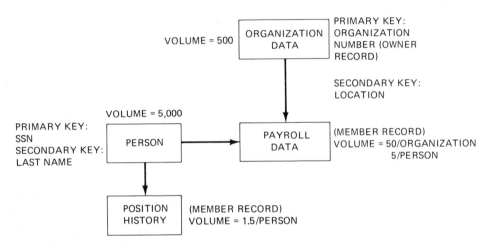

SYSTEM NAME: PERSONNEL SYSTEM
ANALYST: J. JONES
DATE: 12/12/76

Figure 2.   Sample data base structure diagram for a hypothetical system.

2. THE DBA WILL ASSIGN SYSTEM NAMES, DATA ELEMENT NAMES, AND WILL NORMALIZE THE DATA BASE PRIOR TO IMPLEMENTATION. In conjunction with the development of the structure chart, as discussed in the previous section, the systems analyst will provide the DBA a list of tentative data elements for each of the entities shown on the structure chart. In effect, this list of elements by entity constitutes the first normal form of data representation. (Those unfamiliar with reducing data elements to the third normal form should refer to *Computer Data-Base Organization* by James Martin [Englewood Cliffs, N.J., Prentice-Hall, Inc. 1975]). The DBA will carry this normalization process further, until the data have been translated into the *third normal form*. An example of a possible form which can be utilized to assist in this process is shown in Figure 3.

SYSTEM NAME _____

ENTITY NAME _____

FILE NAME _____

APPROVED (DBA NAME) _____ DATE _____

DATA ELEMENT NAME		DESCRIPTION (Purpose)	SPECIFICATION (COBOL Picture)	VOLATILITY
11 Name	Program Designator			

Figure 3.   Sample data element design form.

After reducing the data base to the third normal form, the DBA, along with application analysts, should then list all the plausible changes that might occur to the data base, in order to see how many of them would involve restructuring the data base in such a way, that previously written application programs would have to be rewritten.

3. THE DBA WILL ASSIGN OTHER CRITICAL REVIEW POINTS FOR THE SYSTEM AS REQUIRED. These review points will consist of checkpoints in the specification development process, in order to establish "passwords" and security controls, device/media assignment, JCL review, and other standards. Formal documentation requirements for these review points will be left to the discretion of the DBA, and will depend on the specific system and its complexity.

As a minimum, the DBA will require quality control checks after the detail design specifications have been prepared in the form of a review, and at, or during, the testing phase, to ensure that the actual application software is operating according to standard.

IV. SYSTEM MONITORING

System monitoring functions are primarily concerned with auditing and testing the data base and related software to insure their integrity, security, and adherence to standards. It is expected that a set of specific exception reporting procedures would be developed to assist the DBA in monitoring production systems.   As a minimum, monitoring production systems.   As a minimum, monitoring activities should address:

1. *Time*—The time it takes to run a system (wall clock time, CPU time, response time, etc.).
2. *Space Utilization*—Data base size (on-line space, off-line space, etc.).
3. *Core Requirements*—The amount of core used for production systems, by job or by program.

The precise statistics developed will, of course, depend upon the particular configuration of the installation.   One particularly successful technique, especially in providing information to management, is to present key variables in terms of capacity index.   For example, inline storage capacity might be represented:

$$\text{Online Storage Capacity Index} = 100 \times \frac{\text{On-line Storage Used}}{\text{On-line Storage Available}}$$

Simple, periodic estimates, made on a (monthly) basis, will provide a reasonably easy time series chart upon which forecasts can be made. Other key indexes, which might be of significant use, would be:

1. System response time trends normally expressed as raw data. This is especially useful in spotting inefficient software additions.
2. Wall clock versus execution time for major systems.   Normally useful to isolate systems which might be I/O bound, suggesting restructuring of the I/O requirements.
3. Core utilization index, by system.   Similar to the previous statistic, except this data is useful in checking for inefficient application programs.

These are only a few of many statistical indexes which can be developed to support the system monitoring function.   A key point is, that without such data the DBA is virtually ineffectual in executing the necessary resource changes. With such data, it is often easier to discuss specific problems with non-data processing personnel.   Such documentation will also provide a foundation to development of an effective software planning system.

V. SYSTEM REORGANIZATION

As a result of information gained through system monitoring, or because of new information required in the data base, the Data Base Administrator may have to reorganize the data base. He may:

1. Reassign areas to different devices/media (part of Device/Media Control Language).
2. Change the schema and/or attributes of elements of the schema.

3. Change the data base to reflect the changes in the schema (restructuring).

4. Remove "dead" records and compact space ("garbage collection").

These system reorganization functions are generally concerned with changes to the data base which normally do not affect application programs, and are made primarily on the basis of efficiency of the system. Of the three major tasks identified within the scope of the DBA, this function is the least defined at this point. System reorganization functions will become more critical, and better defined, as the organization of the data base becomes more "mature," larger, and complex.

VI. RECOMMENDED DATA BASE ADMINISTRATOR POSITION DESCRIPTION

The DBA should be a senior member of the data processing organization, who gives an indication of wanting to broaden out in the organization, and who has the appropriate credentials. This individual must rank equal to, or higher than, project managers, and other like individuals, who exert control over the system development process. It is recommended that the individual who is to perform this function be selected as early as possible, in order that the function develop gradually.

The basic qualifications for the position include:

1. *Knowledge of the organization's mission*—A sound understanding of the overall mission will be of significant assistance in long range data base planning.

2. *Skill at negotiation*—The arbitration between users will require a diplomatic, managerial attitude.

3. *Ability to manage data*—Knowledge of data base management systems, data base design, and a thorough understanding of the systems environment is, of course, a key requirement.

4. *Familiarity with operating systems*—A thorough understanding of operating systems characteristics, hardware, and teleprocessing techniques is necessary to make key decisions concerning how the implementation will proceed for particular applications.

The specific tasks, which the individual will perform as a DBA, will consist of:

1. Define the content and structure of the data base.

2. Control data access and search strategies to the data base.

3. Establish data entry standards, maintain dictionary of data elements, research new data elements to prevent redundance, and coordinate definitions of data elements.

4. Maintain accurate and timely documentation of the data base management system, and those portions of the application documentation which pertain to the data base.

5. Exercise proper judgment regarding data base integrity, security, and modification rights.

6. Review the data base structure and its usage, and authorize changes in data base structures as the need arises.

7. Coordinate with project team personnel concerning the data base, as modifications to the operating system and the data base management systems are made.

8. Advise data base users on efficient techniques for extracting data.

9. Keep track of available physical storage, and initiate requests for new devices in sufficient time to meet up-coming needs.

10. Keep apprised of current industry efforts in data base development.

11. Evaluate and/or define possible software modifications, or extensions, to the data base management system.

PRACTICE 0520

DATA BASE REQUIREMENTS DOCUMENT

CONTENTS

I. INTRODUCTION

   A. GENERAL
   B. PURPOSE

II. DATA BASE CONTENT

III. FILE ANALYSIS

   A. IDENTIFICATION
   B. DESCRIPTION
   C. FUNCTIONS
   D. FREQUENCY/ACCURACY
   E. SPECIAL PROCESSING STEPS
   F. CLERICAL/MAINTENANCE
       OPERATIONS REQUIRED

IV. RECORD RELATIONSHIP CHART

   A. OWNS/OWNED BY
   B. RELATED RECORD NAME
   C. RECORD ASSOCIATION METHOD

V. DATA BASE DETAIL CHART

   A. DATA ELEMENT NAME
   B. STANDARD NAME/SYSTEM
       MNEMONIC NAME

C. DERIVATION AND CONTENT
D. MAXIMUM NUMBER OF CHARACTERS
E. DATA TYPE
F. POINTER TO/VALUE
G. FORMAT
H. SIGN POSITION
I. DECIMAL POSITIONS
J. JUSTIFICATION/SYNCHRO-
   NIZATION
K. PREFERRED EDP SOURCE
L. POSSIBLE ALTERNATE SOURCES
M. CREATION METHOD
N. RECORDS IN WHICH DATA
   ELEMENT APPEARS

VI. STORAGE REQUIREMENTS

VII. PROCESSING RESOURCES ESTIMATE

A. CYCLE
B. PROCESSING FUNCTION
C. PHYSICAL I/O's
D. I/O CPU TIME
E. PROCESS CPU TIME

FIGURE1:   DATA FILE ANALYSIS
FIGURE 2:   DATA BASE RECORD RELATION-
            SHIP CHART
FIGURE 3:   DATA BASE DETAIL CHART
FIGURE 4:   PROCESSING RESOURCES FORM

I. INTRODUCTION

A. GENERAL

The data base requirements document is normally prepared when the application uses a file organization, other than purely sequential, with sequential search. This document is prepared by the systems analyst prior to the selection of file organization and access methods.

The general nature of this document is a description of the inter-relationships of data needed by the application (e.g., one field may be used to calculate another, data elements associated to meet an information request).

The document should specify the approach to managing the data, including whether control of the data will be delegated to a data base administrator, a central data control group, or other alternative arrangements.

B.   PURPOSE

The purpose of this document is to understand the relationships that the data elements have to existing documents, and to each other. For applications having hierarchical record relationships, the relationships of different record segments shall be specified.

II.   DATA BASE CONTENT

This section of the document shall specify the data base content required by the application for a batch system; the content shall be organized by input document and/or source of content.

The content analysis in an online system shall be organized by type of processing action. For example, data required to check on shipment status, data required to check on merchandise availability. This data may exist on one or more documents referred to in the course of processing that action.

It shall also be determined what type of recordings will necessarily result from the processing action to be taken. For example, in determining merchandise availability, the control clerk may check the inventory file, and the pending manufacturer delivery file. If the merchandise is not in the current inventory, and new goods are arriving behind schedule, the inquiry status would be "Late shipment, expect delivery in ――― days."

For each processing action, the source of the data shall be identified, such as a specific document or a manual action.

A processing action, or transaction, may stand alone, or be part of a family where the action steps differ, depending on input variations. For each transaction family, a matrix shall be prepared showing the data content and each action within the family. Order entry, for example, may be a transaction family, and the specific action processing logic is based on the type of order. The order processing for custom items would differ from the processing of standard off-the-shelf merchandise.

III.   FILE ANALYSIS

This section shall contain documentation of the general characteristics of the files, present and proposed, to be used in the new system. The Data File Analysis Form (on two sides), illustrated in Figure 1, can be used to collect this information. Instructions for filling in the form are as follows:

A.   IDENTIFICATION

The file name and abbreviated reference tag, if it has one.

B. DESCRIPTION

- *Size*—"10,000 records, five items of data per record."
- *Sequence*—Type and part nomenclature.
- *Media*—"Tub file."
- *Department Location*—"Receiving Department."

C. FUNCTIONS

How the file is used—"Quick reference on different types of parts maintained in stock"

DATA FILE ANALYSIS

IDENTIFICATION

	Tag	File Name
1		
2		
3		
4		
5		
6		
7		
8		
9		
10		

DESCRIPTION

	Size (No. of records and data items per record)	Sequence	Media	Department Location
1				
2				
3				
4				
5				
6				
7				
8				
9				
10				

FUNCTIONS

1	
2	
3	
4	
5	
6	
7	
8	
9	
10	

Figure 1.   Data file analysis form (obverse).

FREQUENCY/ACCURACY

	Frequency of Referral	Frequency of File Updating	Degree of Accuracy of File Data
1			
2			
3			
4			
5			
6			
7			
8			
9			
10			

SPECIAL PROCESSING STEPS

1	
2	
3	
4	
5	
6	
7	
8	
9	
10	

CLERICAL MAINTENANCE OPERATIONS REQUIRED

1	
2	
3	
4	
5	
6	
7	
8	
9	
10	

Figure 1.   Data file analysis form (reverse).

D. **FREQUENCY/ACCURACY**
- How often the file is referred to—"Several times a day."
- How often the file is updated—"Once a month."
- How accurate—"Almost no errors."

E. **SPECIAL PROCESSING STEPS**
Any special file procedures?—"The file is cleansed of parts no longer used whenever a physical parts inventory is taken."

F. **CLERICAL/MAINTENANCE OPERATIONS REQUIRED**
The clerical steps in updating the file.

IV. **RECORD RELATIONSHIP CHART**

In this section, the relationships of the records developed from the various parts of a document shall be recorded, so that the logical access structures of the data base can be tailored to the processing requirements.

An extremely important concept of data base structure is one of sets. A set is a group of records of more than one type, which are interrelated. Each active set has an owner record, and one or more member records. The owner record type is unique within a set, but there may be either one, or many, or each member record type in that set.

A record may be a member of more than one set, and/or the owner of more than one set, and/or both a member and owner of different sets simultaneously.

> For example, in an order entry system, a Ship-to Master Record may own several sets of invoice records, each of which is the owner of the detail line records and the Tax Record, for that particular invoice. The Ship-to-Master is owned by the Customer Master Record. The Sales Tax Record, in addition to being owned by the Invoice Record, may also be owned by the State Sales Tax Collection Record for the state to which goods will be shipped.

Organization:_____   System Identification:_____

Project Name:_____   RECORD NAME:_____

OWNS/OWNED BY		RELATED RECORD NAME	RECORD ASSOCIATION METHOD

Figure 2.   Data base record relationship chart.

To facilitate defining the record ownership relationships, a chart is provided in Figure 2. Instructions for filling in the form are given below:

A. OWNS/OWNED BY
Check the appropriate blank.

B. RELATED RECORD NAME

Enter the name of the record to which this record is related.

C. RECORD ASSOCIATION METHOD

Specify the means by which the system can uniquely identify the record, to which a record is to be connected. For example, each line item in an invoice may be associated to the invoice by including the invoice number in the line item record; or, the Sales Tax Record may be associated with the State Tax Collection Record by virtue of the state field in the Ship-to Master Record.

Note that in plotting the relationships, it is understood that a record's owner, which is also the owner of the set, is implicitly the owner of all the sets of its member records. This relationship need not be charted, because it can be derived by tracing the relationship of the owners or members of the record being examined.

V. DATA BASE DETAIL CHART

In addition to describing data element summary information, a de-. tailed description of each data element that may be used by the system shall be given in this section.

The Data Base Detail Chart (Figure 3) provides a complete and uniform method for gathering this detailed information about each data element. Instructions for filling in the form are given below:

A. DATA ELEMENT NAME

The name by which the data element is known to the data users.

B. STANDARD NAME/SYSTEM MNEMONIC NAME

The data element name found on the Data Base Summary Chart and the mnemonic name developed according to the Identification Standards. (See Practice 0140.)

C. DERIVATION AND CONTENT

A brief description of how the data element is derived; e.g., "Gross Pay = Hours X Rate;" or, the contents of the data element; e.g., "SYSDTE is the current system data on the date of the computer run." This information permits the identification of data elements which are identical except for their names; identification of data elements with the same name, but which are actually unique; and acts as a general aid in system design, implementation, and maintenance.

D. MAXIMUM NUMBER OF CHARACTERS

The *number of characters* shall be specified, including the sign, if it is a separate character, rather than the *amount of computer memory*

1. Data Element Name: _____

2. Standard Name/System Mnemonic Name:

   _____ / _____

3. Derivation and Content: _____

   _____

4. Maximum Number of Characters: _____

5. DATA TYPE (check which):

   ☐ 0 Pointer (direct)   ☐ 3 Numeric   ☐ 6 Alphanumeric
   ☐ 1 Indirect Pointer   ☐ 4 Numeric Edited   ☐ 7 Alphanumeric Edited
   ☐ 2 Date   ☐ 5 Alphabetic   ☐ 8 Literal Value

6. Pointer to / Value: _____

7. FORMAT (check which):

   DATE   NUMERIC

   ☐ 0 MMDDYY   ☐ 0 Character
   ☐ 1 DDMMYY   ☐ 1 Packed Decimal
   ☐ 2 YYMMDD   ☐ 2 Binary
   ☐ 3 YYDDD   ☐ 3 Floating Point

8. SIGN POSITION (check which):

   ☐ 0 Unsigned   ☐ 3 Trailing Separate
   ☐ 1 Leading Separate   ☐ 4 Trailing Overpunch
   ☐ 2 Leading Overpunch   ☐ 5 System Standard

9. Decimal Positions:

10. Justification/Synchronization: _____

11. Preferred EDP Source: _____

12. Possible Alternate Sources: _____

13. Creation Method: _____

14. Records in Which Data Element Appears: _____

    _____   _____   _____
    _____   _____   _____
    _____   _____   _____

Figure 3.   Data base detail chart.

required to contain the data element. This assures consistency and avoids possible confusion. For variable-length data items, the maximum size should be specified.

E. DATA TYPE

The data type of the data element is determined either by the use to which it is put or by its content.

0 *Pointer*—Contains the address or retrieval key of a related record.

1 *Indirect Pointer*—Contains the pointer to a pointer element in another record. The pointer element in the related record may be either direct or indirect.

2 *Date*—Contains a date field in one of the four date formats shown in Item 7 on the Data Base Detail Chart.

3 *Numeric*—Consists only of the digits 0-9 and an optional sign position. It meets the requirements of the vendor's hardware and software, for use as an operand in arithmetic operations.

> Note: For some computers, it may be necessary to add an additional data type for specification of numeric items, except that they cannot be used as arithmetic operands.

4 *Numeric Edited*—A numeric element which also has editing symbols; e.g., "$," decimal point, comma, etc. and which therefore cannot be used as an operand in an arithmetic operation.

5 *Alphabetic*—An element consisting of only the letters A-Z and the character space.

6 *Alphanumeric*—An element which can contain any character in the computer's character set.

7. *Alphanumeric Edited*—An alphanumeric element into which spaces, slashes, or zeros have been inserted as the result of an editing operation.

8. *Literal Value*—The element contains a constant value subject either to no change or to very infrequent change; e.g., the Federal tax deduction per exemption.

F. POINTER TO/VALUE

Contains:

• If a Direct Pointer: the name of the data record type of the record being pointed to.

• If an Indirect Pointer: the name of the data record type of the record being pointed to, and the name of the element in the record which is being pointed to.

• If a Lateral Value: the exact contents of the data element.

G. FORMAT

If a date or numeric element, specify the format of the element shown on the Data Base Detail Chart; otherwise, do not make an entry.

H. SIGN POSITION

If a numeric element, enter the appropriate code; otherwise, do not make an entry. Code 5, "System Standard," should be entered for any numeric format for which there is a vendor standard; e.g., binary numbers are always signed by setting the high-order bits either ON (if negative) or OFF (if positive).

I. DECIMAL POSITIONS

The number of decimal positions in the data element, if it is numeric. "O" should be entered if the element always contains an integer value.

J. JUSTIFICATION/SYNCHRONIZATION

If the data element differs from the system convention, this entry should be made; otherwise, it should be omitted.

K. PREFERRED EDP SOURCE

The point at which the data element can be captured which is closest in location and time to the creation point of the data.

L. POSSIBLE ALTERNATE SOURCES

Alternate sources which may be used in the event it proves impractical to use the preferred data source.

M. CREATION METHOD

How the data is created; e.g., "Copied from customer order;" "Computed based on the wright of the shipment."

N. RECORDS IN WHICH DATA ELEMENT APPEARS

The name of each record in which the same data element appears, regardless of the name by which it is known in the record.

VI. STORAGE REQUIREMENTS

A rough estimate of the data base storage requirements shall be made in this section, although it is not possible to determine accurately the amount of mass storage capacity required, until the logical structure of the data base is selected during the system design phase.

The estimate must allow for space lost to system overhead; e.g., the label cylinder, home address records, and key information space requirements of the operating system and the IOCS routines. In some cases, this loss can amount to well over 10 percent of the available quoted capacity of each disk or drum. In addition to the space lost, due to vendor-imposed limitations, it is also necessary to allow for space lost due to overhead, space required to manage the logical access methods required for the data base.

PROCESSING FUNCTION	I/O's (X 1,000)		I/O CPU TIME (HRS.)		PROCESS CPU TIME (HRS.)		MAIN MEMORY (KILOBYTES)
	AVG.	PEAK	AVG.	PEAK	AVG.	PEAK	
TOTALS							

SYSTEM: DATE:

SUBSYSTEM: PREPARED BY:

CYCLE:

Figure 4.   Processing resources form.

VII.   PROCESSING RESOURCES ESTIMATE

Estimates of the required computer resources within each processing cycle are necessary. The processing functions of each cycle are determined and then, using related input and output volumes, resource estimates are made. For example, there may be 30,000 order transactions and 3,500 shipment inquiries in the daily cycle (these would be run online during the day).

Each night a form (Figure 4) should be completed to provide an inventory status report and to determine whether the computer system is adequate to the total workload. By estimating each cycle, a summary can be prepared for each subsystem's total requirements per period. Instructions for filling in the form are as follows:

A.   CYCLE

Refers to the processing cycle (daily, weekly, etc.) for which the estimates are being made.

B. PROCESSING FUNCTION

This is the list of process names for which process specifications have been completed.

C. PHYSICAL I/O's

This is the estimated number of physical reads and writes required by each processing function.

D. I/O CPU TIME

Refers to the CPU time required to process the physical I/O's indicated, rounded to the nearest hundredth of an hour.

E. PROCESS CPU TIME

This is the estimated processing time for average and peak loading, based on input and output transactions.

F. MAIN MEMORY

Refers to the estimated core needed to run the processing functions identified.

Should this analysis prove insufficient for evaluating system feasibility and cost, the use of simulation may be required to further refine the estimates. This will provide data on the various response times of different workload conditions. For example, the system may be bottlenecking at one point so that the queues become overloaded, and the system crashes because of the heavy load.

Because technical feasibility is being established by this process, review and approval by the technical support staff of these descriptions is necessary.

PRACTICE 0530

DATA DICTIONARY

CONTENTS

I. INTRODUCTION

    A. GENERAL
    B. PURPOSE

II. DICTIONARY CONTENT

III. DICTIONARY FORMAT

FIGURE 1: DATA DICTIONARY

I. INTRODUCTION

A. GENERAL

The data dictionary concept, first developed to meet the needs of management in dealing with the implementation of large MIS systems, has proven a useful and powerful tool for use in the implementation of any data processing system. The data dictionary provides a means of controlling, and monitoring, the use of data elements throughout a system. The existence of a data dictionary tends to prevent naming conflicts within a system and provides a ready source of information about each data element in a system. The scope of the proposed dictionary concept is one dictionary per major application system.

B. PURPOSE

This practice principally defines the format and content of a data dictionary to be used in lieu of a dictionary being available, that is specifically tailored to a particular DBMS.

II. DICTIONARY CONTENT

Each data element used in the system to which the dictionary belongs, shall be described by a standard entry in the dictionary. The entry shall consist of:

SYSTEM	Enter DICT.SS where: SS = System Code
DATA ELEMENT (Full Name)	Each data element shall have a standard name by which it is known and referenced in programs. The full name of the element shall be no more than 31 characters in length and shall comply with the rules for the formation of data names as described in the American National Standard Institute COBOL standard, i.e., the name shall be no more than 31 characters in length and shall start with an alphabetic character.
DATE ENTERED	Insert MM/DD/YR data element is entered into the dictionary.
UPDATED	Insert MM/DD/YR.
DEFINITION	Each entry shall include a definition of the element being described. The definition shall be free form and should be restricted to no more than 5 lines.
FORMAT (COBOL Picture)	Each entry shall include the standard format of the data element in COBOL picture notation.
WHERE CREATED	The name of each program which can create the data element must be specified. The names of programs which update the contents of the data element are considered programs which create the element. The purpose of including both programs which can create the element, and programs which can update the element in this category, is to enable the maintenance programmer to quickly isolate all programs which are capable of modifying the contents of the data element.

WHERE APPEARING
(Data Set(s))

The name of each data set in which this data element appears shall be given. The standard name, as defined in the Job Control Language Standards practice naming conventions, shall be used.

REMARKS

(Optional)

System:_____

DATA ELEMENT
(Full Name)   _____

DATE:
         ENTERED ___/___/___   UPDATED ___/___/___

DEFINITION: _____
                 _____
                 _____
                 _____
                 _____

FORMAT:
(COBOL
 Picture)   _____

WHERE
CREATED:
(Programs)   _____   _____   _____
                 _____   _____   _____
                 _____   _____   _____
                 _____   _____   _____
                 _____   _____   _____

WHERE
APPEARING:
(Data Set(s))   _____
                 _____
                 _____
                 _____
                 _____

REMARKS: _____
                 _____

Figure 1. Data dictionary.

III. DICTIONARY FORMAT

The format is based on using the standard form. A sample of this form is shown in Figure 1.

PRACTICE 0540

DATA BASE ORGANIZATION

CONTENTS

I. INTRODUCTION

    A. GENERAL
    B. PURPOSE

II. DATA BASE CONCEPT AND DEFINITION

III. DATA STRUCTURES

    A. CHAIN STRUCTURES
    B. POINTER ARRAY
    C. LIST STRUCTURE

IV. STRUCTURES COMPARED

    A. COMPLEX CHAIN STRUCTURES
    B. POINTER ARRAYS
    C. HIERARCHICAL POINTER ARRAY STRUCTURES
    D. LIST STRUCTURES
    E. MIXED LOGIC STRUCTURES

V. RECORD DELETION

VI. GARBAGE COLLECTION

VII. RECORD CONTENT DETERMINATION

A. COMMON DATA ELEMENTS
B. COMMON RECORDS

FIGURE 1:   DATA BASE FILE AND
SET RELATIONSHIPS
FIGURE 2:   CHAIN STRUCTURE
FIGURE 3:   COMPLEX CHAIN STRUCTURE
FIGURE 4:   POINTER ARRAY STRUCTURE
FIGURE 5:   HIERARCHICAL POINTER
ARRAY STRUCTURE
FIGURE 6:   LIST STRUCTURE
FIGURE 7:   MIXED LOGICAL STRUCTURE
DATA BASE
FIGURE 8:   DATA ELEMENT COMBINATION
CROSS-REFERENCE

I. INTRODUCTION

A. GENERAL

The data base organization is an exception to other documents in this series, since it is not a specification of procedures and formats. Rather, it is a description of alternative file organizations from which one must be selected. There is the limitation that the data management system used by the installation may not support all methods discussed here, thus limiting the choice.

B. PURPOSE

The data base organization selected shall be documented in pictorial form in order to describe the relationship of the data and associated directories on tables used to locate specific record segments. A narrative description shall accompany the pictorial description to explain the method by which records are addressed or located.

II. DATA BASE CONCEPT AND DEFINITION

A data base consists of collections of related data records, which are organized in a manner which permits access to related records.

Records which are related, but not all of the same type or in the same file, are grouped into sets. A set of related records consists of one *owner* record and one or more *member* records. The owner record may be the only record of its type in the set, but many or all of the member records may be of a common type.

Once access is gained to any record in a set, the data base must permit access to all of the members of the set, regardless of the file to which they belong. Figure 1 depicts the file and set relationships which might be found in the data base for a payroll application. Each set of employee records is owned by the employee master for that employee. Each set consists of the Employee Master File, a Time Worked File of one or more records, and one payroll deduction record for each deduction item.

> Note: In a conventional batch system, these records would be sorted and processed as a group in order to arrive at each employee's net pay. In the data base system, none of the relevant records need be rearranged or moved, and a new record may be added during the processing of a transaction, linking it to other, associated records.

> A record:
> - May belong to more than one set and
> - May be the owner of one or more sets and
> - May be a member of one or more sets.

In the set illustration in Figure 1, the time-worked records may be members of the sets owned by various departments in the organization and used for labor distribution. The deduction records may be members of the sets owned by each deduction master and used to control and report on the total for each of the various deductions.

Once a record is added to the data base, it should not be relocated. Maintenance operators shall be limited to addition, deletion, and the modification of individual fields.

> Note: Although, theoretically, a record can be relocated, it requires the alteration of all pertinent links and pointers.

As a practical matter, the activity required to relocate a record—in all but the most elementary data bases—is too time consuming. Relocation is further undesirable because of the possible problems which could arise if reference attempts were made when records were being relocated.

III. DATA STRUCTURES

There are three basic techniques by which the records in a set may be interconnected:
- Chain structure
- Pointer array
- List structure

A. CHAIN STRUCTURES

A chain structure is one in which each record contains an imbedded pointer to the next record in the group. (A chain structure, in which the last record contains a pointer to the first record in the group, is

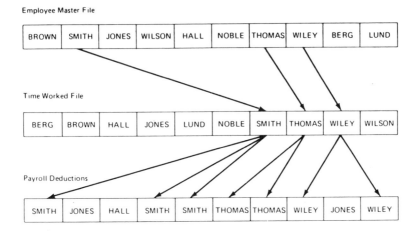

Figure 1. Data base file and set relationships.

a ring structure). A chain structure may be doubly linked instead of singly linked. In this case, each record contains a pointer to the prior, as well as the next, record in the group. Chain structures may be used to link all of the records of one type, all of the records in a set, or whatever records the application requires.

A chain structure, with forward and backward linking, is illustrated in Figure 2. The number in parentheses under each record is its address. In addition to the data which has been omitted, for the sake of clarity, each record contains a record identifier, and the address of the next and the prior record. The logical sequence of a set of records is:

- Customer master
- Invoice leader of the first invoice
- Details of the first invoice.
- Leader of the second invoice

and so on, until all of the invoices and line details for the customer have been linked. The customer master of the next customer follows, and is linked to the last line detail of the current master.

The structure illustrated is a ring structure, because the last record, the customer master for Customer 4, is chained to the first record, the customer master for Customer 1.

> Note: The pointers contain the *address* of the record pointed to, rather than a *key* value. Depending on the restrictions imposed by the mass storage input-output control modules provided by the hardware vendor, the addresses may be either *physical* addresses, or the *relative* position of the record in the file. Relative addressing is preferable to physical addressing, because it permits record sizes to be altered without invalidating the entire data base structure.

If the vendor software supports only physical addressing, a software module, which converts relative addresses to physical address, should be implemented.

CUSTOMER MASTER RECORDS (C)

C1	10	4	C2	9	13	C3	5	15	C4	1	14
CUST	NEXT	PRIOR	CUST	NEXT	PRIOR	COST	NEXT	PRIOR	COST	NEXT	PRIOR
(1)			(2)			(3)			(4)		

INVOICE HEADER RECORDS (I)

I1	16	3	I2	15	20	I3	13	17	I4	11	16	I5	21	2	I6	12	1
INV	NEXT	PRIOR	INV	NEXT	PRIOR	INV	NEXT	PRIOR	INV	NEXT	PRIOR	INV	NEXT	PRIOR	INV	NEXT	PRIOR
(5)			(6)			(7)			(8)			(9)			(10)		

LINE DETAIL (LD)

LD1	22	8	LD2	18	10	LD3	2	7	LD4	4	19	LD5	3	6	LD6	8	5
LINE	NEXT	PRIOR	LINE	NEXT	PRIOR	LINE	NEXT	PRIOR	LINE	NEXT	PRIOR	LINE	NEXT	PRIOR	LINE	NEXT	PRIOR
(11)			(12)			(13)			(14)			(15)			(16)		

LD7	7	18	LD8	17	12	LD9	14	22	LD10	6	21	LD11	20	9	LD12	19	11
LINE	NEXT	PRIOR	LINE	NEXT	PRIOR	LINE	NEXT	PRIOR	LINE	NEXT	PRIOR	LINE	NEXT	PRIOR	LINE	NEXT	PRIOR
(17)			(18)			(19)			(20)			(21)			(22)		

Figure 2. Chain structure (forward and backward linked).

B. POINTER ARRAY

A pointer array, rather than having pointers imbedded in the data records, has independent records consisting only of pointers. If the group can be accessed through only one entry point; e.g., the set of payroll records for an employee can be accessed only through the employee master, the accessing can be either directly to the pointer array, instead of the data record, or to the first record which contains an imbedded pointer to the pointer array. If several records in a set or group can be directly accessed by the user, each record must contain an imbedded pointer to the pointer array.

C. LIST STRUCTURE

The list structure is similar to the pointer array except that, instead of the independent record consisting solely of pointers, it consists of one entry for each record which contains a retrieval key, as well as the pointer to the record.

Pointer arrays and lists may be accessed directly, or through higher-level pointer arrays and lists. In practice, it is also common to find data bases accessed through lists, or pointer arrays in which they, but not the data records, form a chain structure. The permissible combinations of the three structures are limited only to cases in which it is common to find a record which is linked to one set of records by a list structure, or pointer array, and to another set with a chain structure.

IV. STRUCTURES COMPARED

No one of the three structures is superior to the others on an across-the-board basis. Each structure offers clear advantages in some regards, and equally clear disadvantages in others.

With chain structure, it is easier and faster to create or delete an entire group of records, but it is slower and more difficult to insert, or delete, individual records than with either pointer arrays or lists, because of the pointer management requirements. Inserting and deleting individual records from chains with both forward and backward pointers is even more difficult and time consuming. When processing a chain structure, half of the records in the chain, on the average, must be accessed to process a random member of the chain. To dictate a processing sequence, other than the inherent sequence, it is necessary to create a copy of the chain group, or to list *sort,* or to otherwise rearrange it.

A. COMPLEX CHAIN STRUCTURES

A complex chain structure is depicted in Figures 3 and 4 (the data is the same as shown in Figure 3). This is a chain structure in which

CUSTOMER MASTER

CUST NMBR	POINTERS			
	NEXT	PRIOR	INVC	SLSMN
C1	2	4	10	32
(1)				
C2	3	1	9	31
(2)				
C3	4	2	5	31
(3)				

INVOICE HEADERS

INVC NMBR	POINTERS			
	NEXT	PRIOR	CUST	LINE
I1	8	0	3	16
(5)				
I2	0	9	2	15
(6)				
I3	0	10	1	13
(7)				

LINE DETAILS

LINE NMBR	POINTERS			
	NEXT	PRIOR	INVC	ITEM
L1	22	0	8	72
(11)				
L2	18	0	10	73
(12)				
L3	0	0	7	72
(13)				

SALESMAN

SLSMN NMBR	POINTERS							
	NEXT	PRIOR	CUST	CUST	CUST	CUST	CUST	CUST
S1	39	33	3	2	107	110	113	0
(31)								

BILLING ITEM

ITEM NMBR	POINTERS							
	NEXT	PRIOR	LINE	LINE	LINE	LINE	LINE	LINE
B1	0	82	11	13	0	0	0	0
(72)								

Figure 3. Complete chain structure (part one).

CUSTOMER MASTER RECORDS

| CUST NMBR | POINTERS | | | | SALES-MAN |
| | CUST MAST | | INVOICES | | |
	NEXT	PRIOR	FIRST	LAST	
C1	2	4	10	7	32
C2	3	1	9	6	31
C3	4	2	5	8	31

(1)   (2)   (3)

INVOICE HEADER RECORDS

| INVC NMBR | POINTERS | | | | CUST NMBR |
| | INVC HDR | | LINE DETAIL | | |
	NEXT	PRIOR	FIRST	LAST	
I1	8	0	16	16	3
I2	0	9	15	15	2
16	7	0	12	17	1

(5)   (6)   (10)

INVOICE LINE DETAIL RECORDS

| LINE DETAIL NMBR | POINTERS | | | | INVC NMBR |
| | DETAILS | | BILL ITEM | | |
	NEXT	PRIOR	NEXT	PRIOR	
1	22	0	13	17	8
2	18	0	0	15	10
3	0	0	18	11	7

(11)   (12)   (13)

BILLING ITEM MASTER

| ITEM NMBR | POINTERS | | | | DATA |
| | BILL ITEM | | LINE DETAIL | | |
	NEXT	PRIOR	FIRST	LAST	
103	76	92	15	12	

(72)

Figure 3.   Complete chain structure (part two).

many of the records are members of more than one set and, as a result, are linked to more than one record; e.g., the line detail records are also members of the set owned by the Billing Item Master records.

Additional complexity results from the hierarchical structure. In the simple chain structure, all of the records were linked directly to other types of records, while, in the complex structure, each record is linked directly to records of the same type, and by separate pointer(s) to one or more records of different types.

The complex chain structure permits more flexible access than the simple structure, at the expense of additional complexity, when adding and deleting records.

B. POINTER ARRAYS

Essentially, a pointer array is a chain structure in which the pointers have been moved from the data records to independent records. Depending on the number of data records, the pointer array may consist of multiple pointer array records which are chained together, or may be part of a higher level pointer array, or list, structure.

A pointer array structure is more difficult to create or delete than a chain structure, because the pointer array record(s) and the data records must be processed. However, it is generally easier to insert or delete individual records from the pointer array. The insertion or deletion of a record in a pointer array structure is accomplished by writing the record (or adding its address to the free space list) and altering the pointer array accordingly.

The pointer array structure allows access to prior and subsequent records, without the complexity of the forward and backward links required in the chain structure. The space requirement for pointer arrays is generally greater than for a chain structure. Furthermore, the limitations of chain structures, with regard to accessing an array record at random, and working in alternate sequences, also apply to pointer array structures.

The pointer array structure illustrated in Figure 4 contains the same data base depicted in Figures 1, 2, and 3. The structure uses fixed-length pointer arrays. The first pointer addresses the customer master, and the remaining pointers address either invoice headers or line details. Invoice header and line detail records must be read in before they are distinguishable.

C. HIERARCHICAL POINTER ARRAY STRUCTURES

Greater flexibility, and faster retrieval, can be achieved through the use of the hierarchical pointer array structure, such as the one illustrated in Figure 5. Because each level is associated with only one type of record, access to any record type can be predetermined, and the

POINT ARRAY

POINTER ARRAY CUSTOMER 1													POINT ARRAY CUSTOMER 2												
1	10	12	18	17	7	13							2	9	21	20	6	15							

POINT ARRAY CUSTOMER 3																									
3	5	16	8	11	22	19	14																		

CUSTOMER MASTER

CUSTOMER 1	CUSTOMER 2	CUSTOMER 3	CUSTOMER 4
(1)	(2)	(3)	(4)

INVOICED HEADERS

INVOICE 1	INVOICE 2	INVOICE 3	INVOICE 4	INVOICE 5	INVOICE 6
(5)	(6)	(7)	(8)	(9)	(10)

LINE DETAILS

LINE 1	LINE 2	LINE 3	LINE 4	LINE 5	LINE 6	LINE 7	LINE 8	LINE 9	LINE 10	LINE 11	LINE 12
(11)	(12)	(13)	(14)	(15)	(16)	(17)	(18)	(19)	(20)	(21)	(22)

Figure 4. Pointer array structure.

HIGHEST LEVEL ARRAY

POINTERS TO CUSTOMER MASTERS								CHAIN TO POINTER ARRAYS	
CUST 1		CUST 2		CUST 3		CUST 4			
RECORD	ARRAY	RECORD	ARRAY	RECORD	ARRAY	RECORD	ARRAY	NEXT	PRIOR
1	32	2	33	3	34	4	35	0	0

(31)

2ND LEVEL ARRAY

CUST NMBR 1	POINTERS TO INVOICE HEADERS								CHAIN TO POINTER ARRAYS	
	IST INVC		2ND INVC		3RD INVC		4TH INVC			
	RECORD	ARRAY	RECORD	ARRAY	RECORD	ARRAY	RECORD	ARRAY	NEXT	PRIOR
	10	36	7	37	0		0		0	0

(32)

3RD LEVEL ARRAY

INVC NMBR 6	POINTERS TO LINE DETAILS								CHAIN TO POINTER ARRAYS	
									NEXT	PRIOR
	12	18	17	0	0	0	0	0	0	0

(36)

DATA RECORDS

CUSTOMER				INVOICE HEADERS						LINE DETAILS											
1	2	3	4	1	2	3	4	5	6	1	2	3	4	5	6	7	8	9	10	11	12
1	2	3	4	5	6	7	8	9	10	11	12	13	14	15	16	17	18	19	20	21	22

Figure 5. Heirarchical pointer array structure.

time required to access all of the records of one type, is less than the time attainable, using the basic pointer array structure.

D. LIST STRUCTURES

Structures in which the pointers are moved from the data records to a list, and in which data from the record is moved to the list, or duplicated in it, are called list structures. The list entry will include an identifying key, and the address pointer. It may include an indicator of whether the record is the owner, or a member of the set addressed by the list. The lists may be threaded (chained) or unthreaded.

The list structure is comparable to the pointer array structure in speed and ease of creation, or deletion, of the entire structure. It is easier, however, to insert or remove records, because the presence of the key value in the list eliminates the need to access the data records themselves (except in the case of the record being deleted or inserted). The key valve also permits a record to be accessed directly, once the list entry line has been accessed, without having to read any other data records in the group. A sample list structure is shown in Figure 6.

E. MIXED LOGIC STRUCTURES

Figure 7 represents the same data base as in the foregoing examples, but with a mixed logical structure rather than a single structure. Customer master records and invoice headers are accessed through lists, while the line details for each invoice are chains with a forward-backward ring structure.

Chain and pointer array structures are best restricted to situations where all of the records in a group are processed together. A list structure is preferable where records are processed independently, and where all of the records in a group are processed in several sequences.

V. RECORD DELETION

Unlike a physical file, it is common for a data base to be used by several unrelated applications. It is also common for a record pertaining to one application to be deleted from the set(s) of records, while remaining active for other applications (e.g., a year-to-date payroll record for a former employee is deleted from the weekly payroll set, but remains active in the relevant tax-reporting data sets). Since the data base carries only a *single* copy of any record, it is necessary to have a mechanism which can determine the active users of each record, thereby deleting an unused record and saving space. The simplest such mechanism is to reserve the first two characters of each record for a user count. Each time the record is linked into a set, the user count is incremented by one; each time the record is deleted by delinking from a set, it is decremented by one.

LIST RECORDS

Record 1

CUST		ENTRY COUNT													
NMBR	PTR		TYPE	NMBR	PTR	TYPE	NMBR	PTR	TYPE	NMBR	PTR	TYPE	NMBR	PTR	
C1	1	6	1	6	10	L	2	12	L	8	18	L	7	17	

Record 2

CUST		ENTRY COUNT										
NMBR	PTR		TYPE	NMBR	PTR	TYPE	NMBR	PTR	TYPE	NMBR	PTR
C2	2	5	L	3	13	1	5	9	L	11	21

Record 3

CUST		ENTRY COUNT							
NMBR	PTR		TYPE	NMBR	PTR	TYPE	NMBR	PTR	
C3	3	7	L	5	15	1	1	5	

Record 4

TYPE	NMBR	PTR	TYPE	NMBR	PTR	TYPE	NMBR	PTR	TYPE	NMBR	PTR
1	6	16	L	1	11	L	2	12	L	9	19

TYPE	NMBR	PTR
1	3	7
L	10	20
1	2	6
1	4	8

HEAD OF LIST

CUST		
NUMBR	PTR	
−0	14	HEAD OF LIST

CUST		
TYPE	NMBR	PTR
L	4	14

DATA FILE

CUSTOMER

1	2	3	4
1	2	3	4

INVOICE

1	2	3	4
5	6	7	8

LINE DETAIL

1	2	3	4	5	6	7	8	9	10	11	12
11	12	13	14	15	16	17	18	19	20	21	22

Figure 6. List structure.

LIST OF CUSTOMERS

LIST IDENTI-FIER	POINTER		NMBR	PTR	NMBR	PTR	NMBR	PTR	NMBR	PTR
	NEXT LIST	PRIOR LIST								
			C1	61	C2	62	C3	63	C4	64

LIST OF INVOICES FOR ONE CUSTOMER

LIST IDENT	POINTER		PTR CUST MASTER	INVC	PTR	INVC	PTR	INVC	PTR	INVC	PTR
	NEXT LIST	PRIOR LIST		NMBR	PTR	NMBR	PTR	NMBR	PTR	NMBR	PTR
C2	73	0	2	5	9	11	21	10	20	2	6

(62)

INVOICE HEADER AND LINE DETAIL

RECORD IDENT	POINTERS		DATA
	NEXT	PRIOR	
15	21	20	

(9)

RECORD IDENT	POINTER		DATA
	NEXT	PRIOR	

(21)

RECORD IDENT	POINTER		DATA
	NEXT	PRIOR	
LD10	9	21	

(20)

Figure 7.   Mixed logical structure data base.

VI.   GARBAGE COLLECTION

Physically deleting a record from the data base, and making the space available for subsequent additions, is known as "garbage collection". In a data base that contains a considerable number of record areas, and where delete activity cannot occur during peak usage periods, garbage collection may be performed by the program which updates the user count.

> Note: For most data bases, the best approach is to have a single garbage collection program which can be run once a day during a low-activity period. This program physically deletes records with a user count of zero and adds their addresses to a list of available space.

VII.   RECORD CONTENT DETERMINATION

In an off-line system, the file content is dictated by the common source input patterns. In a data base system, the content of the records shall be dictated by common usage patterns. This difference is due to the reduction in number of records and number of record

Element 1					
Element 2	Element 3	Element 4	Element 5	Where Used	Count

Figure 8.   Data element combination cross-reference.

types, resulting from a use-oriented rather than a source-oriented data base.

Unless there are only a few data elements involved in the system, a cross-reference form should be used to analyze and document these relationships. Such a form is shown in Figure 8, and the instructions for filling it in are given below:

- One entry shall be made for each operation performed at each work station.
- Each of the data elements used in the operation shall be arranged alphabetically.
- The element lowest in sequence shall be called *Element 1,* the next lowest, *Element 2,* and so on.
- The work station ID shall appear in the *Where Used* column.
- If the elements are used more than once at that work station, an entry should be made in the *Count* column.
- Additional operations, which have the same Element 1, shall be listed on the same form.

A. COMMON DATA ELEMENTS

Assuming that the new system performs the same operations as the prior system, although differing in technique, and that the same data is required to perform any given operation, the anticipated usage patterns of the various data elements, and their combinations, reflects the grouping of data elements into records.

Many data elements are common to several applications. If record contents are determined solely on common usage, these data elements will be duplicated in the data base one time for each usage beyond the initial usage. Although this will lead to a minimum access time to perform any operation, other than data base maintenance, it also will lead to a loss of speed, and an increase in program complexity in data base maintenance. Yet, each data element can be carried in only one record, in order to expedite data base maintenance, but performance of other data base operations would be degraded.

In addition to finding data elements common among applications, it is typical to find some record types which are common within the same application.

B. COMMON RECORDS

The shifting of common data elements to common records should result in a significant reduction in the number of data elements that are duplicated. Of the duplicated data elements that remain, those which are not subject to maintenance, or change, are of no concern, but those which are likely to need maintenance, require additional consideration.

If the duplicated data element is used in one high-volume, fast-response application, and several low-volume, slow-response applications, the element can be carried only in the record for the high-volume application without any significant degradation in performance. If the duplicated data element is used in several high-volume, fast-response applications, it is preferable to maintain more than one copy of it, unless one of the high-volume applications results in constant change of the data element. It is desirable to have as few duplications as possible, so as to minimize maintenance problems.

SERIES 0600

man-machine dialogue

PRACTICE 0610
DIALOGUE SPECIFICATIONS

CONTENTS

I. INTRODUCTION

    A. GENERAL
    B. PURPOSE

II. DIALOGUE PRIORITIES

III. DIALOGUE DESIGN STRATEGY

    A. CONTROL OF THE DIALOGUE

IV. DIALOGUE STRUCTURE

V. DIALOGUE FORMAT

    A. CRT SCREEN CONVENTIONS
       AND LAYOUT

VI. DIALOGUE VOCABULARY

VII. DIALOGUE SYNTACTICAL RULES

VIII. DIALOGUE CONTROL FUNCTIONS

    A. STANDARD MESSAGES

FIGURE 1: DIALOGUE DESIGN PRIORITIES
FIGURE 2: SAMPLE CRT SCREEN LAYOUT

I. INTRODUCTION

A. GENERAL

The dialogue specification shall be prepared for applications where a man-machine conversation is to occur. This document is primarily a guideline for writing specifications, rather than a tutorial on dialogue design. This practice identifies all the major elements which must be included in a specification, and also provides a guide for tying the specifications to key application requirements.

B. PURPOSE

The purpose of this practice is to define the structure, format, conventions, and controls that are the parameters which describe the man-machine interaction.

II. DIALOGUE PRIORITIES

In this section of the specification, the dialogue design objectives shall be clarified. In order to distinguish the relative importance of different design objectives, a priority ordering of objectives shall be established. In an order entry application, the priority order may be:
   1. Ability to detect errors in stock numbers, quantity, payment provisions, and other essential order items.
   2. Minimize the number of key strokes per transaction.
   3. Minimize the operator training requirements.

The first and second priorities would lead to the selection of a technique which uses mneumonics, special codes, and has the maximum amount of data within one screen page. The third priority would lead to the selection of a more lucid dialogue, such as a question/answer format, with each data field individually entered.

A special form for setting the design objective priority order is shown in Figure 1. After the initial selection, using the form, important priorities (those given a "1") shall be rank-ordered to further identify the critical design objectives.

III. DIALOGUE DESIGN STRATEGY

This section shall describe the strategy to be employed in the man-machine dialogue. Strategy refers to *how* and in *what manner* one will communicate with the machine. The operator may use voice commands with a terminal capable of accepting speech input. On the other hand, he may point to specific items on a list for which he wants further information, using a light pen. Or, he may depress a special function key on the keyboard to initiate a reservation action.

The computer may respond by presenting a form to be filled out

DIALOGUE DESIGN PRIORITIES

Rate the importance of each objective in design of dialogue for this application/transaction. Give brief narrative justification/rationale.	SYSTEM _____ APPLICATION _____ TRANSACTION/ _____ TASK _____	
Priority (1-3)	Objective	Rationale
	• Minimize time to input transaction. • Minimize number keystrokes per transaction. • Ensure completeness of entry. • Minimize operator keying errors. • Minimize number undetected errors. • Minimize operator training required. • Minimize operator time per transaction. • Minimize system response time. • Conversational interaction-like natural language. • Computer initiation/control of interaction. • Operator initiation/control of interaction. • Simplify programming to implement. • Minimize computer time per transaction. • Minimize data base accesses per transaction.	

Figure 1.   Dialogue design priorities.

by the operator, or a list of subjects for which information is available, or with a graph of a mathematical function computed from the operator's input.

Strategy not only involves the *media* (e.g., voice, text, picture) of information exchanges, but also includes the *technique* by which this information will be communicated and who controls the dialogue itself. The operator may use a light pen to point to a particular field on a form for which he wishes to change the data. He may be given a menu of possible data entries from which to choose the one to be entered next. A policeman may radio in information about a suspect (e.g., driver's license number, vehicle license number, etc.) which will, in turn, be entered by a terminal operator in a special information center. If a possible violation is found, an audible alarm may be sounded at the terminal.

A. CONTROL OF THE DIALOGUE

Another aspect of strategy is *operator* versus *computer* control of the dialogue. The method of control or discipline shall be fully described in this paragraph.

Control includes initiation of the dialogue, the ordering of information to be exchanged in the dialogue, the determination of exceptions to normal processing, and termination of the transaction.

In the menu selection approach, the *computer* initiates and controls the entire dialogue. The operator may first be shown the main directory, and asked to select the item of interest. If he selects "incident reports," he is then shown the types of incidents available. Therefore, he is guided by the computer, through a series of directories, to a specific record in the data base.

If an English language type of dialogue were used, then the *operator* guides the search. A typical query might be: Incidents, Northeast, Critical, Reactors, Installed prior to 1964.

Operator-controlled dialogue is preferred over computer-controlled dialogue. Latitude for operator decisions should be built into the dialogue to facilitate his continued attention (e.g., operator controls the sequence in which data items are entered; operator selects next processing action from a menu; operator overrides computer decision).

It is not necessary for the dialogue to be entirely operator or computer controlled. It may be designed so that the operator has the option to control some aspects of the dialogue, while the computer will control others.

This will be illustrated with a dialogue where the computer controls the overall flow, and the operator the specific ordering of data. The dialogue is simple, in that the computer controls the parameters being entered, and the user the specific data fields.

This particular illustration is in the field of real estate. It is an automated multiple listing system. In the manual system, the data on each property is contained on a listing card. In the new system, the data is online, and accessed through a terminal in each broker's office. Sample dialogues are shown in Figures 2 and 3. The computer asks the agent to enter the function desired; SL = Search Listings. Next, the computer asks the class being searched. The agent answers "1," the code for single family. For the features entry, the agent both selects the entries to be made, and the order in which they are keyed into the computer.

Similarly, the agent chooses the key words to be used. In Figure 2 it was only price. In the record example, Figure 3, price and subdivision were the key words. However, there were no matches in the first search so the features requested were limited to four bedrooms, using a combination of letter and number code.

```
ENTER FUNCTION CODE
SL
CLASS?1
TRANSACTION?S
ENTER FEATURES
B1C4,5D4,5I3J1Z4
ENTER KEYWORDS
?LP:72000
?
NO MATCHING LISTINGS STORED IN COMPUTER
SL   COMPLETE
```

Figure 2.   Real estate dialogue (sample 1).

```
ENTER FUNCTION CODE
SL
CLASS?1
TRANSACTION?S
ENTER FEATURES
Z4
ENTER KEYWORDS
?LP:72000
?SD:WEST END PARK
?
MATCHING PROPERTIES FROM OTHER OFFICES

#17039  LNG 1   515 CARR AV          23H12   04/Y2  $70,000    SALE S3C1
  SD:WEST END PARK     LB:L35B18                  MB:$.00      IR:0
  ZP:20850             ON:M/M RYAN     PH:340-8441  CA:$.00     MP:0
  LS:7700              LA:JIM ADAMS    TP:840-1545  MD:99.0     TX:1,239
  AG:14                CR:6                                     TN:0
CHILDREN WALK TO PARKS,MOVIES,STORES,LIBRARY,SWIMMING.LNG HOLDS DEPOSIT
A4B1C6D3E2F1,5G1,4H4I5,7J3K1L1M1N1P102R5S3T2U1,11V1,2,14W1,5,6,8,12,15
X1,2,3Y2Z4

#13420  MTG    509 CARR AV           23 H12  04/Y2  $69,950    SALE S3C1
  SD:WEST END PARK     LB:L32 B18                 MB:$12,000   IR:5.0
  ZP:20850             ON:MAROTTI      PH:762-9531  CA:$69,950  MP:209
  LS:7700              LA:BURTON       TP:774-7302  MD:5.0      TX:1,232
  AG:14                CR:6                                     TN:0
1 YR LTD WARRANTY EXTRA INSUL (LOW UTILS) SHOW PLACE RAMB NR RT 270
A1B1C2,5D5,6E2F1,6G1,3H7I3,5,7J3K1L1M1N1,706P102,7R5S1,7T3U3,10V2,14,15
W1,5,6,10,12,15X1,2,3,6,7,11Y2Z4

#13860  SMR    521 W. MONTGOMERY AV   23H 13  04/Y1  $63,950    SALE S3C1
  SD:WEST END PARK     LB:L9 B2P                  MB:$41,000   IR:9.0
  ZP:20850             ON:MM FRENCH    PH:340-2214  CA:$63,050  MP:407
  LS:50 181            LA:M FRENCC     TP:424-7711  MD:5.0      TX:511
  AG:44                CR:6                                     TN:215
ASSUME SUBJECT LENDERS APPROVAL.HUGE ATTIC COULD BE OTHER BEDROOMS
A5B1C2D3E3F4,5G6H4I3J2K2L7M1N605P102R5S1T4U2,14V7,14W6X6Y1Z4

#11623  MLD    524 BEALL AVENUE       23 H13  04/Y2  $59,950    SALE S3C1
  SD:WEST END PARK     LB:L42 B7                  MB:$18,700   IR:0
  ZP:20850             ON:DRS MATTHEWS PH:340-8145  CA:$59,950  MP:0
  LS:10000ASF          LA:E STEWARD    TP:384-8200  MD:3.0      TX:653
  AG:5                 CR:6                                     TN:226
CONV CLOSE IN A1 CONDITION LG CLOSETSLOW UTILITIES
A2B1C2D4,6,7E4F7G1,3H5I1K1,4L1,4M1N1,603,4P102R3,4,5S3T4U3,12,14
V3,8,9,14,15W1,4,5,6,10,12X1,2,3,6,11Y2Z4

#15790  CCI 11 803 WEST MONTGOMERY    23G13   04/Y2  $54,990    SALE S3C1
  SD:WESTEND PARK      LB:L37B4                   MB:$23,800   IR:8.0
  ZP:20852             ON:SMITHFIELD   PH:340-9367  CA:$.00     MP:26,910
  LS:4902              LA:C.SEGESMAN   TP:942-9000  MD:99.0     TX:745
  AG:29                CR:7                                     TN:0
A5B1C2D2E3F5G1,6H4I3J1K2L7M1N105P102,7R3,5,7S1T2U14V2,14,15W5,10,12X1,2
Y2Z4
SL   COMPLETE
```

Figure 3.   Real estate dialogue (sample 2).

IV. DIALOGUE STRUCTURE

The dialogue structure may be defined as the protocol by which the man and the system exchange information. This protocol shall be described in this section in a manner similar to the three examples given below:

A. The operator requests a particular form.
- The computer performs the edit checks, encodes the display with special characters, and transmits the form back to the CRT.
- The operator observes that certain fields are blinking (those with errors) and makes the appropriate corrections.
- The operator transmits the form to the computer.
- The computer repeats the edit checks.
- The computer enters the transaction into the data base and sends an acknowledgement.

B. The bank manager requests information on the status of outstanding loans.
- The computer determines what was requested by looking up the code number in a type request table.
- The computer retrieves the appropriate menu and transmits it to the CRT.
- The operator reads the menu and points (the CRT has a touch-sensitive front panel) to a topic—outstanding loans by state.
- The computer determines the topic selected, and retrieves a states list and transmits it to the terminal.
- The operator selects a state—Alabama.
- The computer determines the state and retrieves from the data base the outstanding loan data.
- The manager views the data, using a scroll feature (which provides for additional lines of data to be added to the bottom of the screen).

C. The technician requests a training program on the operation of a new copy machine model.
- The computer retrieves the first page of the lesson material and transmits it to the CRT.
- The technician reads the lesson material and pushes the SEND button to request the next page.
- The technician answers the multiple choice questions (on the material previously presented) and sends the test answers to the computer.
- The program scores the test and determines that the technician does not understand the character of the reduction mechanism.
- The computer selects the remedial instructions from storage and transmits it to the CRT.
- The technician studies the lesson material and answers affirmatively regarding his readiness for reexamination.

- The computer analyzes the technician's reply and re-presents the test to the technician.
- The technician completes the test, and sends it to the computer.
- The computer scores the test, and sends the technician immediate feedback of the test results.

V. DIALOGUE FORMAT

The type of input format to be used shall be documented in this section, with examples shown as they would appear on the screen. A choice must be made between a fixed-form input and a free-form input. A fixed format is basically a form where an operator is asked to fill in blanks. There are many different types of free-form inputs. Some examples are:

1. ITEM NUMBER: 7257, QTY: 10 tons, GRADE: A.
2. ON WHAT SUBJECTS DO YOU WISH INFORMATION?
   ENTER EACH SUBJECT ON A SEPARATE LINE:
   History, IBM.
   Comparison 1970-75 with Standard & Poors.
   Best performers 1974 New York Stock Exchange.

The system recognizes key words (e.g., History, Comparison, Performers) and interprets the request.

A. CRT SCREEN CONVENTIONS AND LAYOUT

The specifications for information display shall be given in this section. Standard conventions shall be established for the application. Some examples are:

1. Transaction heading shall be displayed on the third line, fifth position from the left margin.
2. Additional explanations and other types of prompting shall be displayed on the bottom five screen lines.
3. Transaction acknowledgements shall be displayed in the upper right-hand corner of the screen.
4. Home position of the cursor shall be on line four, left-most position (the point to which the cursor will return when the home key is depressed).

A screen layout(s) shall be created for all fixed-format type dialogues. This screen layout shall specify the position of the cursor (if set by the computer in preparation for operator response).

If a field protection feature is to be used, indicate with brackets the fields to be protected. Use upper and lower case printing, as will appear on the CRT screen (e.g., computer responses in the upper case, and operator responses in the lower case). A sample CRT screen layout form is shown in Figure 4. The cross-hatched areas indicate a border, which is to be left blank.

VI. DIALOGUE VOCABULARY

The constraints and limitations of the allowable vocabulary shall be specified in this section. The vocabulary may be limited to a few key words, such as a set of action commands (e.g., create, modify, display, save, retransmit), or allow unrestrained natural language input. The dialogue may allow some restrained form of natural language speech, where the unnecessary words (e.g., the, be, a, of, in) are eliminated in the input message processor.

In some dialogue designs, provisions are made for saving unrecognizable words. These words are later considered for inclusion in the updated application dictionary.

VII. DIALOGUE SYNTACTICAL RULES

For those dialogues using an English language format, the rules for making data entries shall be described. These rules involve delimiters between data fields, the use of field separators between data entries, and punctuation at the end of a line entry or transaction.

Example:

Operator Entry: DELIMITER   TOTAL QUANTITY   END LINE INDICATOR

STOCK = 1720 / QUTY - 1000/ /

COLOR = BR 100 # RD 500 # GRSR 400 / /

         COLOR   QUANTITY   FIELD INDICATOR   ROOF

Computer Response:

CHEVETTE, RALLEY MODEL
    BROWN 100
    RED   500
    GREEN 400
TOTAL ORDER = 1000
IF CORRECT ENTER OKAY BELOW
? OKAY

VIII. DIALOGUE CONTROL FUNCTIONS

This section shall contain specifications for system and application control mechanisms that are to accompany the programmed flow of the dialogues. These control functions shall be designed to make the man-machine interaction comfortable and natural.

The principal categories of the controls are:

- *General References and Assistance*—Additional explanations of

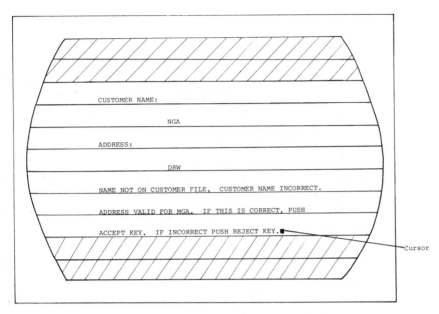

Figure 4. Sample CRT screen layout.

transaction messages, dictionary look-up of applications terms, assistance with terminal operations.

- *Status*—Information on system utilization, such as the number of users online, transmission line availability, terminal status, remaining storage availability, system response times.
- *Transaction Control*—Operator direction of the conversation, such as:
  1. Save the transaction for later return.
  2. Return to current transaction.
  3. Abort the transaction.
  4. Initiate the printout.
  5. Display the current transaction.
  6. Return to earlier display page.
  7. Return to previously stored transaction.

The above controls functions enable the operator to interrupt the transaction and return to it at his discretion. The operator may wish to check with the data base administrator regarding the validity of a certain data entry.

Controls 5 and 6 would be used in a complex multi-page transaction, where the operator would wish to review decisions on previous pages.

A. STANDARD MESSAGES

A standard set of messages shall be defined for common processing conditions that pertain to the system, or the individual application transactions.

Some examples are:

1. SYSTEM WILL BE UNAVAILABLE FROM ___:___ TO ___:___ . PLEASE PARDON INCONVENIENCE.
2. DISK SPACE IS CURRENTLY UNAVAILABLE. PLEASE TRY LATER.
3. PLEASE REENTER MESSAGE. TRANSMISSION PROBLEMS.
4. RECORD NOT FOUND ON MASTER FILE. RECHECK TRANSACTION KEY.
5. IDENTIFICATION CODE NOT RECOGNIZED. PLEASE SEE SECURITY OFFICER.
6. TRANSACTION OKAY.
7. (Field name) FAILS EDIT CHECKS. PLEASE SEE OPERATOR.
8. (Field name) FAILS EDIT CHECKS AGAIN. TRANSACTION NNN PLACED ON HOLD.
9. REQUEST TOO GENERAL. WOULD PRODUCE NNN PAGE RESPONSE. ENTER AGAIN. BE MORE SPECIFIC.

SERIES 0700

data communications

PRACTICE 0710

COMMUNICATIONS REQUIREMENTS DOCUMENT

CONTENTS

I. INTRODUCTION

    A. GENERAL
    B. PURPOSE

II. TRAFFIC SURVEY

    A. COMMUNICATIONS NETWORK NODE
       SELECTION
    B. COMMUNICATIONS NETWORK TRAFFIC
       SURVEY RECORDS
    C. TRAFFIC ANALYSIS

III. NETWORK TOPOLOGY MAP

IV. SERVICE REQUIREMENTS

    A. SERVICE INTERRUPTABILITY
    B. TRANSMISSION ACCURACY
    C. RESPONSE TIME REQUIREMENTS

V. TELECOMMUNICATIONS DATA
    COLLECTION

FIGURE 1: NETWORK NODE SELECTION
           CHART
FIGURE 2: TRAFFIC SURVEY RECORD
FIGURE 3: AVERAGE HOURLY
           MESSAGE VOLUME

FIGURE 4: SEASONAL VARIATION IN
DAILY MESSAGE VOLUMES
FIGURE 5: TRAFFIC DISTRIBUTION BY
TIME OF DAY (AVERAGE
WEEKDAY)
FIGURE 6: TRAFFIC DISTRIBUTION BY TIME
OF DAY (PEAK WEEKDAY)
FIGURE 7: TRAFFIC DISTRIBUTION BY DAY
OF THE WEEK
FIGURE 8: TRAFFIC DISTRIBUTION BY POINT
OF ORIGIN
FIGURE 9: TELECOMMUNICATIONS DATA
COLLECTION FORM

I. INTRODUCTION

A. GENERAL

The communications requirements document shall be prepared whenever an application will require the use of remote facilities in a teleprocessing mode. This technical document is a guide for the analysis of the application's communications requirements, in terms of the traffic that will be generated by that application, and for the analysis of traffic patterns.

B. PURPOSE

The purposes of this document are to define communications traffic loads which the system must handle, and to minimize the traffic workloads in a form suitable to network design.

II. TRAFFIC SURVEY

This section shall describe the methodology used in conducting the traffic analysis survey. In particular, it shall describe the source of data, the method of data collection, and the duration. If the message traffic volume was stabilized through the use of a sampling technique, then the procedure for selecting particular locations to be sampled, should be described. (See the form shown in Section V.)

A. COMMUNICATIONS NETWORK NODE SELECTION

A chart shall be prepared, which describes the proposed network locations, including the locations of nodes and specific locations of terminals, if known. Figure 1 is an illustration of a traffic survey node selection chart. Selected fields in the form are:

- *Network Node*—Metropolitan area at which there will be a line drop or a terminal central unit.

Network Node	State	Loca-tion	Transaction	Special Requirements	Comments
Chicago	IL	B-10	Credit control/ordering	Chicago store open 15 hr/day	
Chicago	IL	G-20	Inv. control	-	
Abiline	KS	B-15	Credit control/Ordering	-	Opens 7/1/76
Abiline	KS	B-20	Credit control/Ordering	-	
Charlevoix	MI	S-12	Credit control/Ordering	-	Marginal store-- only one in northern part of state.
Detroit	MI	S-22	Credit control/Ordering	-	
Detroit	MI	S-13	Credit control/Ordering	-	
Detroit	MI	S-50	Sales Analysis	-	

Figure 1.   Network node selection chart.

- *Location*—Identification of the building in which the terminal will be placed.
- *Transaction Identification*—Types of transactions or messages which will originate from the location specified (e.g., credit authorization).

B. COMMUNICATIONS NETWORK TRAFFIC SURVEY RECORDS

This section shall contain the results of the traffic survey, recorded on appropriate survey forms. This will insure the integrity of the traffic data. An illustrative form for counting individual messages is shown in Figure 2. Selected fields are as follows:

- *Origin*—The specific location from where the message, or document, if the present system does not use electronic media, is sent.
- *Time*—The time period during which messages are counted.
- *Message Name*—Each type of message shall be clearly identified, since several types of messages may originate from the same location.
- *Destination*—The point to which the message, or document, is sent (e.g., regional office).
- *Number of Messages*—Clarify whether messages are being counted, or transactions, since there may be multiple messages for one transaction.
- *Message Size*—This field is completed only if the size of the message varies considerably from message to message.

The purpose of this form is to avoid confusion as to whether data refers to messages transmitted or received. Also, it avoids confusion on the figures that refer to transaction or message, keeping in mind that one transaction may have several messages.

ORIGIN:
Node_____
State_____

TIME:		DATE	DAY OF WEEK	MESSAGE NAME	DESTINATION	NO. OF MESSAGES	MESSAGE SIZE (CHARACTERS)
From	To						
:	:						

Figure 2.   Traffic survey record.

C. TRAFFIC ANALYSIS

This section shall summarize the survey data to make it useful for network design. Average message volumes and anticipated peak traffic loads shall be recorded. The pattern of the workload over-time must be understood. For example, peak usage may occur between the hours of ten and twelve in the morning and three and five in the afternoon, on Mondays through Thursdays. Usage on Friday, Saturday, and Sunday may be extremely light. The message traffic levels may drop of substantially from the end of May to mid-September.

Summarizations for the patterns of message traffic, relevant to specific applications, shall be recorded. Traffic survey data may be used to develop average traffic volumes, peak traffic volumes, and anticipated total traffic loads over time.

The following traffic summarizations are representative of those that shall be prepared:

- Average Hourly Message Volume (Figure 3.)
- Seasonal Variations in Daily Message Volumes (Figure 4)
- Traffic Distribution by Time of Day (Average weekday) (Figure 5.)
- Traffic Districtution by Time of Day (Peak weekday) (Figure 6.)

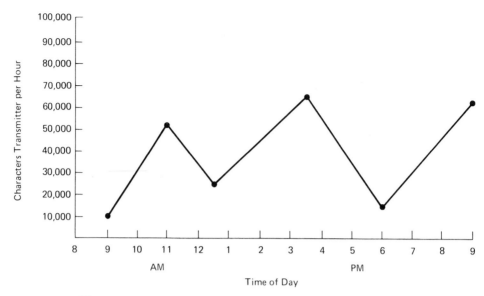

Figure 5.   Traffic distribution by time of day (average weekday).

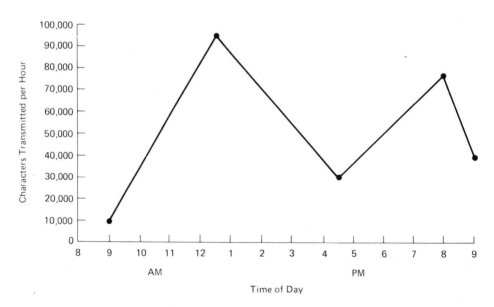

Figure 6.   Traffic distribution by time of day (peak weekday).

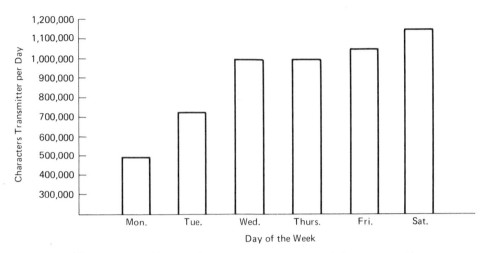

Figure 7.   Traffic distribution by day of the week (average week).

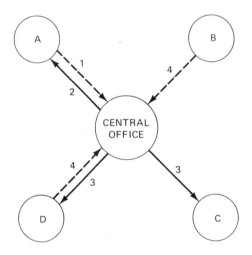

"From" Site	Message Type	"To" Site	No. Messages
B	4	Central Office	100
A	1	Central Office	50
Central Office	2	A	200
D	4	Central Office	1000
Central Office	3	D	500
Central Office	3	C	400

Figure 8.   Traffic distribution by point of origin (average daily).

III. NETWORK TOPOLOGY MAP

A network topology map shall be drawn, which shows the locations of terminals, transmission facilities, and special communications equipment. A legend such as the following shall be used:

Central Computer

Data Concentrator

Terminal Control Unit

Modem

Half Duplex

Full Duplex

LL   Leased Line

DN   Dial-up Network

IV. SERVICE REQUIREMENTS

This section shall describe the application requirements in terms of:

A.   SERVICE INTERRUPTABILITY

A leased line may be less expensive than the dial-up alternative. However, line outages can occur, interrupting customer service.

B.   TRANSMISSION ACCURACY

If transmission accuracy is important, as is the case with systems dealing with quantitative data, this must be documented. Fewer transmission errors occur with specially conditioned lines than with unconditioned lines.

C.   RESPONSE TIME REQUIREMENTS

The requirements of the system, in terms of maximum time delays, must be clearly stated (e.g., the time required for the operator to get the attention of the central computer). Response time delays can occur if a line is unavailable, or all ports are busy at the central computer.

V. TELECOMMUNICATIONS DATA COLLECTION

The type of system to be used determines the nature of the data to be gathered for a particular telecommunications system. The form shown in Figure 9 is used to gather data on the number of transactions, and the number of sites, for each type of application. This data can be used to define and configure particular telecommunications networks, and to define lines and concentrators to meet user needs most cost effectively.

To economize on line costs, several terminals can use a common line in most inquiry and retrieval telecommunications systems. An important consideration is the application's requirement for response time; for example, a delay of 18 seconds versus a delay of 3 seconds, to achieve the correct line loading of terminals per line.

For correct line utilization calculations, it is also important to determine the amount of line traffic, and the transaction's length. Information for collecting transaction volumes for line loading is contained in Part 2 of the form. Information for obtaining data on projected transaction volume, and geographic requirements, is contained in Part 3. To determine the quantity of online storage needed for telecommunications applications, and the amount of CPU processing needed to access this information, see Part 4. A means of summarizing particular operational requirements for specific applications (such as reliability, up-time, and backup requirements) is provided in Part 5.

OUTLINE FOR COLLECTING DATA FOR TELECOMMUNICATIONS DESIGN

Filled Out By: _____

Date:_____   Application _____

1. *SUMMARY DATA*

No. Remote Sites _____

No. Transaction/Day Peak _____

No. Transaction/Hour Peak _____

Allowable Response Time (Seconds) Min _____ Max. _____

2. *TRANSACTION DETAILS*

Transaction Type	No. Transactions Per Day	Average No. of Characters Per Transaction	Maximum No. of Characters Per Transaction
_____	_____	_____	_____
_____	_____	_____	_____
_____	_____	_____	_____
_____	_____	_____	_____
_____	_____	_____	_____

Figure 9.   Telecommunications data collection form.

3. *LINE AND TERMINAL CONFIGURATION ESTIMATING DATA*

No. of Sites Anticipated _____

Total Distance of all Sites from Existing CPU (estimate) _____

No. of Terminals Per Site (Estimate) _____

ESTIMATED NUMBER OF TRANSACTIONS BY SITE

Site	No. of Transactions	No. of Terminals

4. *FILE ACCESSING REQUIREMENTS*

Types of Data (or Files) To Be Accessed (Updated)	Estimated Size of File Characters	No. of Accesses Per Transaction	No. of Transactions	No. of Accesses Total

TOTAL

5. *OPERATIONAL REQUIREMENTS*

No. of hours per day system must operate from _____ to_____ hrs _____

Allowable length of unscheduled down time,   _____

Required terminal and circuit reliability   _____

Maximum amount of training per operator (day)   _____

Hard copy needed?   _____ Yes/No

Backup Requirements_____ All Data

_____ Last week's data only

Figure 9.   Telecommunications data collection form (cont.).

PRACTICE 0720

COMMUNICATIONS SPECIFICATIONS

CONTENTS

I. INTRODUCTION

    A. GENERAL
    B. PURPOSE

II. DESIGN CONSIDERATIONS

    A. DISTRIBUTED VERSUS CENTRAL
       PROCESSING
    B. SHARED NETWORK
    C. TRAFFIC CONCENTRATION
    D. NETWORK LAYOUT
    E. SERVICE
    F. ERROR DETECTION/CORRECTION

III. COST ANALYSIS

    A. COST-EFFECTIVENESS

IV. NETWORK CONTROL

V. COST ESTIMATION

VI. TELECOMMUNICATIONS DESIGN

    A. SOFTWARE
    B. HARDWARE

FIGURE 1: TYPICAL CONFIGURATION OF A
            REMOTE CONCENTRATOR

FIGURE 2:   SPIDER WEB COMMUNICATIONS
             NETWORK
FIGURE 3:   SPIRAL PATTERN COMMUNICATIONS
             NETWORK USING MULTIDROP
             LINES
FIGURE 4:   MULTI-POINT MILEAGE DE-
             TERMINATION
FIGURE 5:   CONCENTRATOR NETWORK
FIGURE 6:   COST ESTIMATION FORM
FIGURE 7:   TELECOMMUNICATIONS SOFTWARE
             REQUIREMENTS FORM
FIGURE 8:   TELECOMMUNICATIONS HARDWARE
             REQUIREMENTS FORM

I. INTRODUCTION

A. GENERAL

A communications network specification shall be prepared for all applications. The basic focus of this practice is on the factors in designing the network that will produce a minimum cost solution, compatible with service requirements.

B. PURPOSE

This document is written to provide specifications for the data communications network including the equipment configuration, network topology, transmission facilities, and network control software.

II. DESIGN CONSIDERATIONS

This section shall document the various design alternatives to be considered for the data communications function.

A. DISTRIBUTED VERSUS CENTRAL PROCESSING

This section shall discuss the option of using a distributed processing approach to reducing communications costs. If the performance of applications processing functions can substantially reduce long distance communications traffic, this may result in significant cost savings.

B. SHARED NETWORK

If one application will not provide sufficient line-loading to make the communications network cost-effective, then the possibility of sharing the network with other applications shall be investigated and documented in this section of the document.

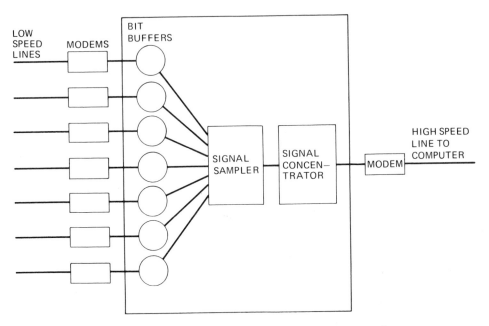

Figure 1.   Typical configuration of a remote concentration.

C. TRAFFIC CONCENTRATION

The concentration of traffic on the network shall be recorded in this section, in order to determine the need to use a data concentrator to reduce network costs.   Traffic from a number of low-speed devices, using low-speed lines, may be condensed and transmitted to the computer on a single high-speed line, as illustrated in Figure 1.

The cost for the high-speed leased line, and the data concentrator, may be significantly less than the cost of separate leased lines to the central computer site.

> Note: Network simulation programs, which can calculate the optimum location of the data concentrator, are available.

D. NETWORK LAYOUT

The geographic dispersion of the network shall be studied according to the following criteria:

1. *Even distribution of the workload among the lines.*
   A situation where the line loading on one line is only 20% of total capacity, while the loading on another line is 80% of capacity, should be avoided.   Figure 2 is an example of a poor line pattern.   Figure 3 shows a better arrangement, where a number of stations are connected to one common carrier.

2. *Minimizing the total number of circuit miles.*
   The optimal network layout is one that will provide the least

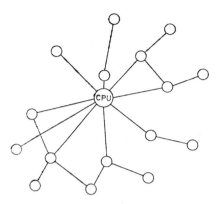

Figure 2.   Spider web communications network.

number of circuit miles. A number of alternative layouts shall
be developed, and the mileage under each alternative shall
be measured. Figure 4 is an example of mileage determination
for a simple multi-point network.

3. *Arranging the circuits so that alternate routings are available.*
A simple means of improving network reliability in complex
network structures is line redundancy, where alternative line
paths are available.

Note: The probability of a concurrent failure of two disjointed leased lines is about
one in a million.

For most business applications (e.g., order entry, credit inquiry),
line redundancy is not warranted. Line outages will be so infrequent that the added cost is not justified.

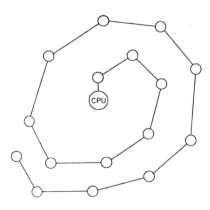

Figure 3.   Spiral pattern communications network using multidrop lines.

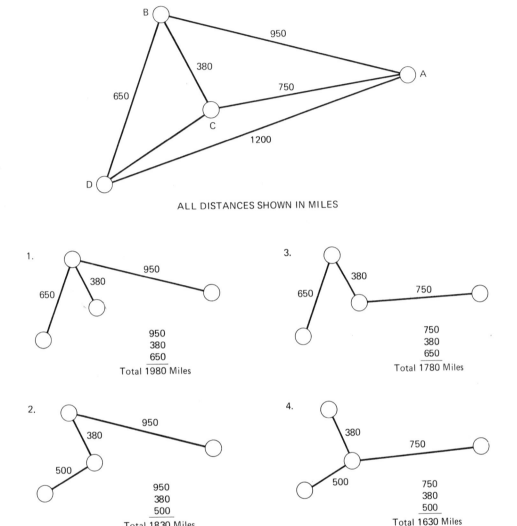

Figure 4.   Multi-point mileage determination.

E. SERVICE

This section shall discuss adequate service levels, in terms of response time and reliability, which are consistent with service cost limitations. Line and port availability are the determining factors in response time. The designer must trade off cost against delays in obtaining service during peak periods. Network costs can be significantly reduced, if a several minute delay can be tolerated during peak periods. A customary ratio of terminals to ports ranges from 5 to 1 and 10 to 1.

The principal factors in reliability are line conditioning, and a network switching mechanism.

A discussion of public versus private networks should be included. The dial-up (public) network is less reliable than a private network, in terms of transmission of errors, because it uses unconditioned lines. It is also less desirable than the private network, because mechanical switching devices create a noise disturbance. The dial-up network is more reliable in terms of line availability, since it has a nearly endless network of alternative paths.

> Note: Many private communications networks use the dial-up network as a backup facility.

F. ERROR DETECTION/CORRECTION

An error detection and correction strategy shall be developed, in keeping with the accuracy requirements of the application. This section shall describe various error detection schemes, which will keep the number of undetected errors within tolerable limits.

In a typical conditioned leased voice grade line, one bit in 100,000 will contain an error. If the error detection scheme is able to catch 9 out of 10 errors, then only one out of one million bits would have an undetected error. For most applications this is not a severe problem, since it is easy for an operator to recognize a garbled message, or the computer edit routines to identify the field as having an error.

III. COST ANALYSIS

This section shall contain a computation of the total costs for alternative network designs. The cost of modems, lines, line drops, and special communications equipment shall be included in computing these costs.

If a design requires the purchase of special communications equipment, then a 10-year amortization schedule shall be included.

Line charges are based on a sliding scale, which is based on distance (e.g., $3/mile/month for the first 25 miles, and the next 75 miles at $2.10/miles/month).

Under the tariff schedules, the users must pay an additional charge for each station of the multidrop line. A typical charge is $12.50/month for the first drop and $7.50/month thereafter.

A. COST-EFFECTIVENESS

This section shall calculate cost savings that would result from the use of special communications equipment.

1. *Modem Sharing Unit (MSU)*—A device that connects several terminals (up to 6) to a single modem.

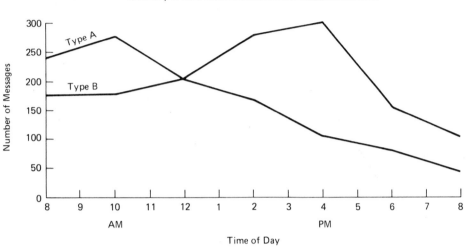

Figure 3.   Average hourly message volume (by type and time of day).

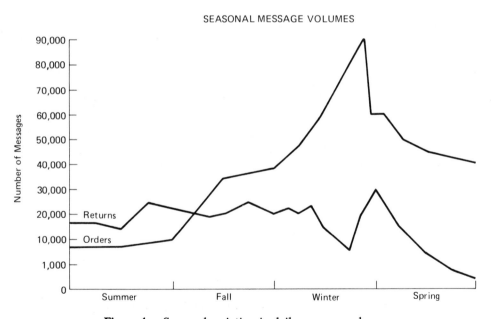

Figure 4.   Seasonal variation in daily message volumes.

- Traffic Distribution by Day of the Week (Average week) (Figure 7.)
- Traffic Distribution by Point of Origin (Average Daily) (Figure 8.)

Note: Information received by the MSU is broadcast to all terminals, and the first terminal to respond appropriately gains access to the MSU.

In a location having four terminals, each requiring a 2400 baud modem, there would be a monthly saving of three modems plus line drops, minus the cost of the MSU.

2. *Multiplexer*—A multiplexer is a device used to divide the bandwidth of a facility into several segments, each serving as a separate channel. One voice grade facility may have the channel capacity of several low-speed lines, and provide cost reductions on the order of 50%.

3. *Concentrator*—This device is used to condense data traffic on low-speed lines to a single high-speed line. This effectuates cost savings, because there is less total circuit mileage.

Note: A concentrator output channel capacity must be greater than the sum of the average data rates of the terminals connected to its input ports. A concentrator may perform such local operations as polling, error checking, and line control, as well as transferring information to the computer with efficient high-speed transmission techniques.

An example of a network which uses concentrators is shown in Figure 5.

NETWORK DESIGN

CONCENTRATOR NETWORK

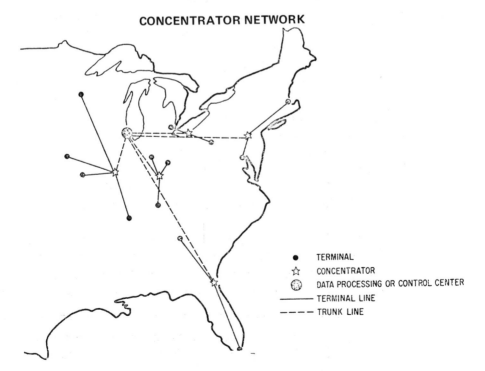

TERMINAL
CONCENTRATOR
DATA PROCESSING OR CONTROL CENTER
TERMINAL LINE
TRUNK LINE

Figure 5. Concentrator network.

4. *Port Sharing Unit*—A device for connecting several modems to a single computer or concentrator port. It operates in a manner analogous to the MSU. Its cost-effectiveness is determined by comparing it with the cost of adding equipment to the central computer.

Front-End Processor (FEP)— A special computer at the central site that interfaces the communications network with the central computer's CPU.

Note: The overhead requirements for a large CPU, to interact with many communications lines at modem levels, is too great to be economically attractive.

The FEP performs the same task as a concentrator, but with the purpose of efficiently utilizing the I/O channel of the CPU.

IV. NETWORK CONTROL

This section shall document the methods and logic used in the control of a telecommunications network. If a package is used, such as CICS, the relevant specifications shall be extracted from the package documentation for use by the applications programmer. Suggested items to be included in these specifications are:

1. *Line Control*—The discipline by which the message traffic will be controlled, if a polling system is to be used. The polling sequence and method are specified.
2. *Error Detection and Correction*—Action to be taken when an error is detected (e.g., "Request one re-transmission. If the message is still garbled, inform the system controller of communication link problem.")
3. *Queue Management*—Description of management technique including maximum queue size. Procedures to be used during traffic overload conditions.
4. *Priority Assignment*—Description of priority levels to be used, and the logic by which a priority will be assigned..
5. *Message Logging*—The procedures used for creating a backup file for Restart and Recovery. Message logged content shall be described (e.g., line identification, security control reference, message copy).
6. *Message Control*—This procedure is used to control the message to be processed. Message sequence numbers are given, to assure that the sequence is maintained correctly; messages are held in a ledger, and are not released until the transaction is completed.

   Note: This permits a message to be cancelled at any time during the proceedings.

7. *Message Format*—A standardized message format shall be adopted for all transactions. A simple format is shown below:

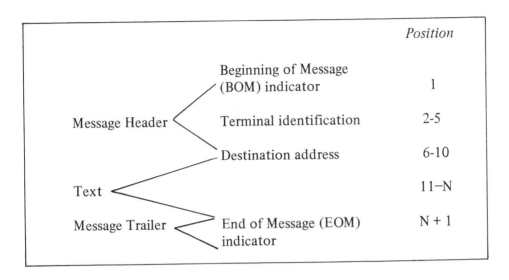

		Position
Message Header	Beginning of Message (BOM) indicator	1
	Terminal identification	2-5
	Destination address	6-10
Text		11–N
Message Trailer	End of Message (EOM) indicator	N + 1

V. COST ESTIMATION

During the preliminary design phase, each time the telecommunications network is reconfigured, costs must be re-estimated. Although each specific design will have unique characteristics, general aspects are illustrated in the form shown in Figure 6, which shall be included in this section of the document.

It is helpful to make standard estimates, where possible, to make calculations easier. While approximations for some costs suffice during the preliminary design phase, more accurate figures should be sought for any aspect of the system that involves a major portion of the total cost.

The number and length of what kinds of lines will be used to connect what kinds of concentrators, is often not so easy to evaluate. This is also the most important aspect in arriving at an efficient design. In the early design phase, general estimates may be made by placing concentrators on maps in seemingly appropriate places, and then using rule of thumb calculations of costs and line loading. The particular application will determine the degree of accuracy required in this determination.

Since the transaction's complexity is unknown, (for example, the number of files to be accessed) CPU estimates are difficult to make. However, a 4 ms per transaction on large processors (such as a 370/155) is a ballpark figure. Serial file accessing is rapid: .2 ms, and complex data base accessing can require 20 ms CPU time on a 370/155. Estimate the rate per hour at the commercial billing rate for a 370/155.

An estimate of disk costs may be made, based on the chosen file storage device type. Core costs are determined by assuming that most line controlling packages use approximately 200,000 characters of space, and that each line requires a certain quantity of core for buffers.

COST ESTIMATION

TERMINALS AND CONCENTRATORS

Terminal Type	Quantity	Cost Per Unit Mth	Total Cost
Remote Batch			
CRT			
Typewriter			
Concentrator			
TOTAL			

LINE COSTS

Line Type	Miles	Per/mile/Mth	Cost
Wide Band (50 Kilo Baud)			
Voice Grade Leased Leased			
Voice Grade Switched			
Narrow Band (150 Baud)			
TOTAL			

Figure 6. Cost estimation form.

Naturally, these figures differ with the system used; however, they are given as logical estimates. It is recommended that the rate per hour of core be illustrated in a table.

VI. TELECOMMUNICATIONS DESIGN

The forms contained in this section involve documenting the type of data which results from a telecommunications design task. The documentation for each of the many types of telecommunications systems

MODEMS

2 Per Link

Line Type	Number Links	Price/Mth	Cost
Wide Band (50 Kilo baud)	_____	_____	_____
Voice Grade Band (9,600 Baud)	_____	_____	_____
Voice Grade (2,400 baud)	_____	_____	_____
Slow Speed (300 baud)	_____	_____	_____
_____	_____	_____	_____
_____	_____	_____	_____
_____	_____	_____	_____
TOTAL			_____

CPU ESTIMATES

Total number transactions x 4 ms CPU = _____

_____ CPU time x $500/hr = _____

DISK STORAGE COSTS

Online Characters	Disk Pack Charges	Cost/Mth
_____	_____	_____

Core Costs

Assume 200 K characters + 1K per line = _____ K

   On a large machine

_____ K x cost of core x _____ hrs/mth available = _____

SOFTWARE PACKAGES

Name	Cost/Mth
_____	_____
_____	_____
_____	_____
_____	_____
TOTAL	_____

TOTAL MONTHLY APPLICATION COST   _____

Figure 6.   (Cont., page 2).

is significantly different. Emphasis is placed on the documentation needed for a fairly slow speed line network of keyboard terminals. Portions of this documentation, and documentation unique to other systems can be used to describe other types of remote processing, such as process control, or remote job entry.

These forms should help in assuring that the pitfalls of telecommunications design are known, before the process of systems coding and testing is begun. Therefore, the forms contain inquiries about the handling of file lockout and file recovery. However, the form does not contain provisions for documenting file formats on a character-by-character basis.

A. SOFTWARE

The kind of application, and its related functions, should be identified in the general design, and included in this section. The applications programs should be flowcharted, and documented during the detailed design phase. Specific problems related to telecommunications systems are identified in this section. The anticipated response time for each transaction type is identified in Section 1 of the form shown in Figure 7. This response time is the sum of transmission times through all of the system's links, delays through line loading in each link, and processing delays in the central site, because of computer file accessing and CPU loading. Every transaction is dependent upon acess to particular files related to that application. Contingent on their indexing scheme and file organization, each of these files may demand several accesses.

One major factor in arriving at the total transaction processing time is the speed of these accesses. The slowest case response time can be accessed by utilizing rule of thumb figures, related to the particular hardware of the proposed installation.

Terminal communications and line error recovery often use packages. The designer should clearly understand, and relate to, the programmer the types of error conditions encountered, and the kinds of corrections obtainable through particular packages. This exchange of information is crucial to a clear understanding of what may be obtained by using the package, and what must be written by the programmer.

Included for cross reference is the application program documentation section of the form.

Section 2 on the form, File Interfaces, shall be documented with consideration given to the particular problems that will evolve from online telecommunications systems.

The file recovery system and its operation should be defined. A key problem in telecommunications systems is, that if the system crashes immediately after an operator has entered a transaction, he might be unsure as to whether or not a particular update to a file was properly processed before the response was lost. If file updating does not take place at the terminals, recovering the response will be greatly facilitated. In this way, the only recovery required is that an offline copy be present to reestablish the file.

Security is an important concern for most remote communication systems. Computer file rooms can be more easily locked than can terminal rooms, which must be more accessible. Some of the means that limit the accessibility to certain data are: logs of users, passwords, and limitations of file access by specific applications. Another method is to permit only special users to write on certain files, allowing others only access privileges.

The rapidity of processing transactions is greatly affected by indexing techniques used for online files. If more than one indexing code is permitted for inquiry to a given file, these indexing patterns are more complicated. In most instances, indexing necessitates extra time or accesses beyond those needed to logically obtain a given record from a

TELECOMMUNICATIONS SOFTWARE REQUIREMENTS

SYSTEM: Date:

SUBSYSTEM: Prepared by:

1. TRANSACTIONS AND INTERFACE TO APPLICATION PROGRAM

Type of Transaction	Length of Input	Length of Response	No./Hr. peak period	No. Disk Accesses per Transaction	Maximum Response Time Expected

Describe:

1. Interface application program and terminals.
2. Standard error conditions and responses (if a package is used).
3. Operation of special routine to handle the interface housekeeping.

_____
_____
_____
_____
_____
_____
_____
_____

Figure 7.   Telecommunications software requirements form.

Line Recovery

Describe: Package _____

User written _____

_____

Message Queue length: _____

Total disk/core space: _____

Priority: _____

_____

_____

APPLICATION PROGRAM DOCUMENTATION

The documentation of the flow of the application programs should
follow normal program documentation procedures. Please record
cross reference between modules below:

Name	Description	Files Accessed
_____	_____	_____
	_____	_____
	_____	_____
_____	_____	_____
	_____	_____
	_____	_____
_____	_____	_____
	_____	_____
	_____	_____
	_____	_____

Give core, CPU, and file cost estimates so they may be used to
derive total telecommunications costs.

PROCESSING COSTS/MONTH: _____

2. FILE INTERFACES

Is each transaction which can change an online file separately

logged? _____

When are online files copied to off-line storage for backup?

File	Backup Schedule (Weekly, Daily, etc.)
_____	_____
_____	_____
_____	_____

Describe recovery process for a software failure that loses
transaction queue's:

_____

_____

_____

_____

Figure 7. (page 2).

```
Describe recovery process for lost online files (head crash):
```

_____

_____

_____

_____

File Interfaces

```
The basic file structure is defined in the documentation of files.
Specific questions that must be addressed for online files.
```

```
Specific indexing techniques
```

File Name	Indexing Scheme	No. Physical Access/ Logical Access	Time to Access
_____	_____	_____	_____
_____	_____	_____	_____
_____	_____	_____	_____

```
Security Requirements   (User password, partial elements of the
file, by application).
```

_____

_____

_____


```
Describe lockout scheme for any files which could possibly be
updated simultaneously (by record, by file, etc.).
```

_____

_____

_____

_____

Figure 7.   (page 3).

file.   Therefore, the number of logical records retrieved may be exceeded by the number of physical accesses to a data base.   In this portion of the form, the data documented is helpful in determining the transaction response time of the first portion of the software section.

The problem exists that several users may simultaneously want to update the same physical piece of data, in any kind of file that is updated from a remote location.   The methods for file lockout are an important consideration in this classic problem, the "deadly embrace." Some file accessing methods will lock out all other users from a file, allowing only one user to access the file at one time.   Used by batch processing multiprogramming environments, this method is unsatisfactory if there are a great number of remote users all trying to access the same file.   Superior methods will lock out a specific record that is being accessed by a particular user from any other user accessing that specific record.

TELECOMMUNICATIONS HARDWARE REQUIREMENTS

SYSTEM:	Date:
SUBSYSTEM:	Prepared by:

1. TERMINALS AND MODEMS

Terminal Brand & No.	Site	Quantity	Price/ Month	Modem Name	Modem Price/ Month	Total Cost
————	————	————	————	————	————	————
————	————	————	————	————	————	————
————	————	————	————	————	————	————
————	————	————	————	————	————	————
————	————	————	————	————	————	————

2. TOTAL LINES

Line Type	Half/Fall Duplex	Conditioning	From	To	Miles	Cost/Month
————	————	————	————	————	————	————
————	————	————	————	————	————	————
————	————	————	————	————	————	————

Long Distance and WATS Charge Estimates: ————

TOTAL/MONTH ————

3. CONCENTRATORS, FRONT END PROCESSORS, MULTIPLES

Unit	Memory Size	Peripherals	No. Ports	Modems	Features	Price
————	————	————	————	————	————	————
————	————	————	————	————	————	————
————	————	————	————	————	————	————
————	————	————	————	————	————	————

TOTAL HARDWARE COST/MONTH: ————

Figure 8. Telecommunications hardware requirements form.

The kind of software to be used in the concentrator, or a front-end processor, should be included in the software documentation for telecommunications design. The only documentation needed for vendor-supplied software is that provided by the vendor. For recovery routines, and for creating backup files, the software required should be documented as parts of the needed modules to run the system. The recovery and backup schedule should be closely connected with the updating of a file from transactions. Thus, carefully considered design in this area is important. The same process used to establish a backup file may be used for efficient batch processing against the same file, through skillful design.

B. TERMINAL HARDWARE

The choice of basic terminal types is the result of the general design process.   During the detailed design phase, each device should be described in detail in this section, including features and expected costs.   Figure 8, which documents hardware requirements, includes the description of terminal features, and the lines and the concentrators needed in the system.   Special features, such as interrupt keys, link control device, and character sets should be noted.

PRACTICE 0730
TERMINAL REQUIREMENTS DOCUMENT

CONTENTS

I. INTRODUCTION

    A. GENERAL
    B. PURPOSE

II. TERMINAL FEATURES

III. HUMAN ENGINEERING

IV. OPERATOR CHARACTERISTICS

V. TERMINAL CHARACTERISTICS

VI. TERMINAL REQUIREMENTS CHECKLIST

    A. GENERAL
    B. FORMAT CONTROL
    C. SCREEN CHARACTERISTICS
    D. CONTROL FEATURES
    E. MAINTENANCE AND RELIABILITY

VII. KEYBOARD DESIGN

    A. KEYBOARD CONTROLS
    B. EDITING FEATURES
    C. CURSOR CONTROL
    D. CHARACTER SET
    E. OTHER

I. INTRODUCTION

A. GENERAL

The terminal requirements document shall be prepared for all transaction-oriented applications. This document is prepared by the systems analyst, with close coordination with user personnel, who are familiar with the human factors which are particular to the application. These factors will be translated by the analyst into terminal requirements that will smooth the man-machine interaction.

B. PURPOSE

The purposes of this practice are to present information regarding device types, speed, features, keyboard functions, and layout, and to record user characteristics. Specific devices, available features, and their costs are also to be recorded.

II. TERMINAL FEATURES

This section shall describe the features of various terminals, and shall include cost comparisons. A basic choice is between a typewriter-like device and a CRT. A disadvantage of typewriter-like devices is that they operate at lower speeds than a human is capable of reading; however, they are less expensive than a CRT.

Note: A teletype can be purchased for under a thousand dollars, while the least expensive CRTs are over two thousand dollars.

Both device types are available with a wide variety of features. All of these features should be examined in terms of specific application requirements. A teletype device with a lower case may be needed for a credit collection application in which "personal letters" would be written to delinquent accounts, for example.

A teletype with an upper and lower case, however, costs nearly as much as a CRT. A CRT has the advantage of editing features which are associated with an erasable screen. The credit representative would use the editing features to insert a message into the standard text. A special printing device would have to be attached to the CRT to produce the hard copy letter to the customer.

The analyst must have a clear idea of the application requirements in order to separate *imagined* needs from *real* needs. Unfortunately, the lead time requirements for ordering hardware are such, that the analyst will be forced to make an early decision.

III. HUMAN ENGINEERING

In this section, the conditions under which the terminal will be used, shall be documented. Some suggested factors are:
- Number of hours spent at the terminal per day.

- Noise level of the environment in which the terminal operator will have to act.
- Time required at one sitting.
- Employer and/or user expectations of time needed to complete a transaction.
- Number of hours per day that the terminal will be used.
- Amount of wear and tear that the device must endure.

If users find the terminal unwieldy, they will avoid its use. The terminal keyboard may be so sluggish that experienced typists find it unsatisfactory for touch typing, or the keyboard may not have special keys for repetitive operator functions (e.g., STORE, SAVE, REQUEST).

The operator frequently may wish to store the current transaction, ask for assistance (HELP key), or perform some similar action, which has to be repeated many times throughout the day. If the operator is not provided with a special key, he will have to repeatedly type in the command.

Eye strain and fatigue may be a problem with long periods of CRT use. This problem may be alleviated by the purchase of a non-glare screen.

IV. OPERATOR CHARACTERISTICS

In this section, the characteristics of individuals who will be using the terminals shall be described. An order entry application, using skilled typists, has different requirements than does an information retrieval application involving physicians, who are impatient to get on with their primary duties.

A key factor in developing terminal specifications is, who will be permitted to use the system. In a library retrieval application, the analyst must decide whether professional librarians or students, will have access to the terminals. If the librarian is the only one permitted to use the device, the keyboard can be specially engineered to reduce the number of key strokes per information request.

Some human characteristics to consider are:
- Attention to detail
- Manual dexterity
- Concentration level
- Attitude towards machines
- Feelings about the work
- Coolness under pressure

V. TERMINAL CHARACTERISTICS

In this section a list of device types shall be given, from which a selection can be made. A suggested list is:
- Keyboard-like typewriter
- Push-button telephone

- Light pen
- Voice input
- Voice output
- Touch panel
- Point-of-sale terminals
- Badge/credit card reader
- Magnetic tape cassette
- Optical document reader
- Mark-sense reader
- Plotter
- Non-impact printer
- CRT character display
- CRT vector display

Data volumes, type of transactions, requirements for hard copy, and the nature of the output response, should be documented. For some applications, a voice answer-back coupled with a push-button telephone input, may satisfy the application requirements.

Initially, the analyst should search for a general type terminal that is best suited to the application. In an order entry application, in which visual verification of order entry is needed, a CRT is preferred over a typewriter terminal.

When the device type has been selected, other considerations, such as cost, reliability, and performance, come into play. Secondary decisions involve the specific configuration (e.g., a non-impact printer with a cluster of four CRTs), and device features (e.g., the system automatically activates the terminal and receives data without the operator being present). An alarm may be needed to alert the operator that information (e.g., an announcement) is about to be transmitted from computer to terminal.

No one factor, such as cost, should dictate a terminal choice. In selecting the terminal type, and features, it is important to distinguish between "nice to have" and "required" terminal capabilities. A graphic CRT is desirable for displaying trend data, but these trends could be just as well displayed in tabular form, on a typewriter terminal.

VI. TERMINAL REQUIREMENTS CHECKLIST

This section shall contain a checklist to be used by the analyst to round out the terminal requirements specification, after a device type(s) has been selected.

A. GENERAL
- Intelligent (programmable) terminal
- Data transmission rate
- Transmission mode (full duplex, half duplex, simplex)
- Transmission code; e.g., ASCII

- Error detection capability
- Automatic dial-up capability
- Built-in modem
- Logic for multi-drop line operation
- Automatic answering capability
- Number of terminals connectable to a control unit
- Memory capacity
- Automatic retransmission in case of error

B. FORMAT CONTROL
- Field protect (prohibits the operator from overstriking data)
- Automatic skip to next field

C. SCREEN CHARACTERISTICS
- Protection from external glare
- Number of displayable characters
- Number of lines
- Number of characters per line

Vector capacity
Highlighting
- Linking
- Colors
- Different levels of brightness
- Reverse field (background and characters)
- Variations of character size

Screen addressing method
- Blocks
- Split screen
- Individual positions
- Line

D. CONTROL FEATURES
- End of page warning
- Console status light
- Local versus remote switch
- Audible alarm (for unattended terminal)

E. MAINTENANCE AND RELIABILITY
- Mean time to failure of terminal components (e.g., CRT tube, light pen, keyboard, printing mechanism)
- Modularity of design

VII.   KEYBOARD DESIGN

This section shall describe the design of the keyboard.   Keyboard design is often virtually ignored because the design of the data base communications network seems to take precedence. In one case, the installation of an entry system was delayed for six months, and $20,000 was spent to reengineer it, because the original keyboard was not laid out for use by a touch typist.

It is critical that the man-machine dialogues be sufficiently well-defined, so that special keyboard functions are known. Typically, functions that may be used are:

- HELP
- REQUEST
- UPDATE
- DELETE
- EXPLAIN

The analyst must determine whether one set of predefined keyboard functions will be made standard, or whether a keyboard with provisions to overlay different templates will be required. A labeled plastic overlay template is placed over the keys, each having a unique combination of holes. The template transmits a coded bit pattern to the terminal service program, which is used to search a special table, which identifies the specific application. One template may be used for inquiry, another for data entry, and a third for a data file audit.

If a CRT has been selected as the terminal, there are special keyboard considerations, in conjunction with data entered and displayed on the screen. If forms are to be filled in, a vertical and horizontal tabulation key will be needed, to facilitate the movement of the cursor to various fields on the form.

Another is that of different character fonts for special applications (e.g., personalized dunning letters). A number of CRTs provide programmable character sets, in conjunction with a keyboard with interchangeable keys.

Provisions for security shall be considered (if the keyboard can be locked so that the keys cannot be depressed) under system controls to thwart unauthorized access. If passwords are to be required, a non-printing feature, or display suppression feature, will be required.

Other aspects involve whether the terminal can operate in an unattended mode. The following checklist should be included in this section, for review when preparing the keyboard specifications:

A. KEYBOARD CONTROLS

- Scroll feature
- Reverse tabs
- Screen clear
- Skip new page
- Carriage return
- Vertical tab

- Horizontal tab
- Line feed

B.   EDITING FEATURES

- Character erase
- Character insert
- Line erase
- Line insert

C.   CURSOR CONTROL

- Destructive cursor
- Non-destructive cursor
- Cursor home key (uppermost left position of screen)
- Light pen (as pointing device for cursor movement)

D.   CHARACTER SET

- Interchangeable fonts
- Printing versus non-printing characters
- Upper-lower case
- Superscripts
- Subscripts

E.   OTHER

- One-hand operation
- Lockable keyboard (under program control)
- Cancel transmission key

INDEX

COBOL
  Data Division, 68
  program format, 71
COBOL, structured
  CASE, 113
  constructs, 113
  Environment Division, 67
  Procedures Division, 68
completeness check, 81
concentrator
  data, 231
  software, 240
chain structures, 188, 191
construct
  DOUNTIL, 72
  DOWHILE, 72, 113
  IFTHENELSE, 72-113
cost-benefit, 7, 20, 21
cost-estimate
  computer related, 22
  design of network, 223
  network, 233
  personnel-related, 21
  request form, 8
  See also estimate
count-test, 80
CRT layout, 209

DBA, 161
  duties of, 164
  See also data base administrator
data analysis, telecommunications, 202
data base, 13
  graphical representation, 164
  lockout, 239
  logical organization, 164, 188-199
  record ownership, 174
  reorganization, 167
  requirements, 172
data base structure
  logical, 164
  pointer array, 178
data concentrator. *See* concentrator
data correlation and documentation (DCD)
    system, 120
data dictionary, 182
data elements, 177
  cross-reference, 199
  description of, 59
data file description, 185

data requirements, 171
data structure
  chain, 188-189
  complex chain, 191
  hierarchial pointer, 194
  list, 191, 196
  pointer, 191
  pointer array, 191, 194
deadly embrace, 239
dialogue, 204-211
  control functions, 210
  control of, 206, 210
  display conventions, 209
  protocol of, 208
  rules of, 208
  structure of, 208
dialogue design, objective of, 205
documentation
  aids, 101
  program summary, 63
  system design notebook, 56
  terminal operation manual, 150
  terminal requirements, 243

editing
  error analysis, 77, 82
  rules, 76
  self-checking, 77
  validating procedure, 75
estimate
  accuracy of, 10
  hardware usage, 37
  network costs, 233
  processing resource, 181
  resource requirements, 36
  See also cost estimate
estimation, resources, 34
error
  messages, 157
  verification of, 81
error analysis. *See* editing
error detection, network, 232

feasibility study, 11, 14
file analysis, 172
file definition, 91
flowchart, structured, 86, 112
function
  commands, 153
  keys, 153

functional hierarchy, 58

hardware
  terminal characteristics, 244
  terminal keyboard design, 246
  See also terminal
hash, totals, 80
hipo
  detail diagram, 59
  diagram, step-by-step preparation of, 115
  guideline for, 103
  overview diagrams, 58
  short form, 114-115

JCL, 16
  hints, 142
  naming conventions in, 16
job control language. *See* JCL
JCL conventions
  DD statement, 138
  EXEC statement, 136
  format, 134
  job statement, 135

layout, CRT, 209
life cycle, 52
line control, 232
list structure, 191
lockout, 239
  mutual, 239

maintenance
  aid, 124
man-machine dialogue, 204-211
  See also dialogue
manpower estimate, 5, 9, 10
message
  control, 232
  format, 232
  logging, 232
  volume depiction, 219
methodology, structured, 48
multiplexer, 231

naming conventions, 17
network
  design of, 227
  node selection, 217
  mileage, 227
  See also telecommunications

operations manual. *See* production control
  runbook
operator, human factors, 244
online; batch vs., **xii**
output, report, 89

personnel costs, 21-22
pointer array, 191

processing
  costs, 23
  costs estimate, 23
  resource estimate, 80
program
  design, aid in, 122
  format, 70
  format, COBOL, 71
  libraries, 140
  self-contained, 70
  structure, COBOL code, 71
programming, structured, 69
product planning, 3
production control runbook, 145-149

recovery data, 236
request form, cost estimate, 8
resource, utilization, hardware, 97
response time, 222, 236
  review. *See* system review
runbook, preparation of, 146

security, telecommunications of, 237
self-checking, 77
software, life cycle, 52
source listing, annotation of, 121
storage estimate, 179
structured design, 48
  principles of, 46
structured development, 45
structured programming
  guideline for COBOL, 64-73
  prohibition of, 72
  self-contained, 70
system
  design, network traffic, 226
  reorganization, 167
  requirements, study of, 54
  testing, 14
  test-plan, 98
  summary, current, 83
system review
  consisting of, 116
  content of, 115
  critical, 166
  formal, 49
  functional accuracy, 117
  implementation, 117
  in-process, 49

telecommunications
  analysis, 48
  design forms, 234
  traffic description, 220
teleprocessing. *See* telecommunications
terminal
  features of, 243
  keyboard controls, 247
  operator, 150
  requirements checklist, 245

terminal procedures
  SIGN-OFF, 152
  SIGN-ON, 152
testing
  approach of, 78
  content of, 79
  format of, 79
  logical relationship, 78
  strategy of, 99
  system test plan, 98
  unit tests, 78
traffic, survey of, 216-218
trouble-shooting, procedure, 154

user
  interview form, 85
  request, 4

virtual table of contents (VTOC), 58
volume estimates, 90, 94

walk-through, structured, 49
workplan, 13